BURNS
FOR
BAIRNS

and

Lads an' Lassies
an' a'

A selection of poems
suitable for Bairns, Lads and Lassies
selected and annotated
by
Irving Miller

FTCL, FLCM, LGSM, LTCL (Eloc)

Illustrated by
Margaret Irving Miller

First published in 1990 by
Alloway Publishing Ltd.
Second Edition, 1994
revised by James A. Mackay
Reprinted
2003
2004
2007

This edition with revised illustrations by Margaret Irving Miller
published 2014 by Alloway Publishing
an imprint of Stenlake Publishing Limited,
54-58 Mill Square, Catrine,
Ayrshire, KA5 6RD

Tel: 01290 551122
e-mail: enquiries@stenlake.co.uk
www.stenlake.co.uk

ISBN: 9780907526964

The publishers gratefully acknowledge the support of the Royalty Burns Club.

Preface

Although the Greenock Burns Club organised a children's competition for the recitation of the poems of Burns so long ago as 1806, interest in the rich heritage of Scots vernacular poetry in general, and the poems and songs of Robert Burns in particular, is a relatively modern phenomenon. It was not until the turn of the present century that other Burns clubs began to emulate their Greenock cronies. In 1902 six clubs in the West of Scotland organised educational work among schoolchildren, and by the eve of the First World War some 42 Burns clubs were engaged on this vital project.

Out of this pioneering work eventually grew the Schools Competitions which have been organised by the Burns Federation since 1912. Today well over 100,000 children enter these contests each year. While there is a scope for essays, paintings, and individual and group projects, undoubtedly the bulk of the interest is expressed in verse recitation. Over the course of many years the Burns Federation published or sponsored a series of three *Scots Readers* and more recently an admirable anthology of Scottish verse entitled *A Scots Kist*. These books have been out of print for several years and consequently there has been a long-felt need for a replacement.

The vacuum has now been filled by Irving Miller, than whom there can have been few people better qualified and experienced in the field of teaching the elocution of the Scots vernacular. Certainly if one ever had the pleasure of hearing the poems of Burns recited by a trained verse speaker, the lyrical cadences and texture of the Scots Tongue, together with the poems written by Burns in English, both so rich in character and sincerity of thought would be fully appreciated.

I can commend this work, whether for the use in the home, the club or the classroom. Irving Miller carefully graded and selected the poems to suit each age-group and provided invaluable assistance and advice in the speed and mode of delivery to be adopted in each case, drawing attention to the points to be emphasised or dramatised.

James A. Mackay

A WORD TO THE BAIRNS

You already know many poems by Robert Burns, our national bard. In this book you may find some you may not have heard before.

Burns wrote in our Lowland Scots language, and also in the speech you use in your English lessons at school.

There are poems and parts of longer poems in each of these languages. This will give you a wider knowledge of the poetry of one of Scotland's greatest poets. I hope you will find them interesting and you will want to read more from the great number of poems and songs left to us by Robert Burns. Many of these have been translated into many foreign languages, making him famous worldwide.

To help you when reciting, there is a wee note to help you find the mood, the character or the meaning of each poem and the accompanying illustration shows scenes or characters from the poem.

Burns had a keen ear for music and he wrote poems to suit old Scots tunes. If you would like to sing the verses with their lovely words and thoughts ask your teachers and parents to help you find the tunes. There are many books of the songs of Robert Burns.

I hope you will find much to interest, and to enjoy, in the following pages.

Irving Miller

FOR THE LADS AN' LASSIES

During my career as an adjudicator of verse, Burns classes were usually limited to a few well-known poems in Lowland Scots. But Burns also wrote many poems in standard English and some of these are included here to provide a more comprehensive knowledge of the poetry of our national bard.

For Burns Clubs who arrange competitions and those who compile the syllabi for Burns classes in verse speaking in speech and drama at the many festivals throughout the country, the following suggestions may be suitable.

For the bairns classes two contrasting short poems could be used, in different speech and mood, thus displaying the ability of the candidate to speak in each idiom. This ability can be shown in the longer poems chosen for the lads and lassies where Burns inserted verses in English carrying the mood and pace, highlighting each idiom. The speaker by this device can appreciate Burns's many coloured palette of words, rhythms and moods.

Parents and teachers must support the children in their study of the poetry of Burns by discussing the poem and considering what persuaded Burns to write it and why; how he used different forms for presenting his ideas to one person, or many, and where he indulged in the lyric to convey his innermost thoughts.

Many words in Lowland Scots may not be known by the student. There is a marginal glossary alongside each poem giving the meaning.

With each poem there is a short note stating its form and giving advice as to how it should be presented. If the students are interested in singing, encourage them to find the tunes in the "Songs of Burns" of which there are many editions.

There are many different forms of poetry. Burns used them all, from the Rhyming Couplet to one named after him, the Burnsian Stanza, used for example in "To A Mouse". These different forms are explained in the following notes.

I hope you will want to learn more about Robert Burns, his poems and his songs.

Irving Miller

Some Short Notes on Form

Lyric: In Lyric Verse or a song in words, for example, 'The Posie' the poet is speaking his thoughts. Do not intrude. No gestures are needed, only facial expression and emotion.

Narrative: A narrative poem tells a story, for example 'Tam o' Shanter'. This poem is subtitled 'A Tale'. Tell it as a story. Few gestures are needed, take the audience into your confidence, laugh with them and enjoy the humour. Do not give a highly dramatic performance.

Ballad: A Ballad tells a story. More gestures can be used as there is more than one character speaking, for example 'Tam Lin'. It is a swift moving poem. The scene can change in each verse, from shore to sea, from castle to battle. Many characters in many moods and emotions are presented.

Epistle: An Epistle is a letter in rhyme. Burns wrote many in the Burnsian Stanza. They should be spoken with a picture of the poet at his desk writing. No gestures. When studying Burns for recital remember the basic elements of good speech.

Rhyme & Rhythm: These make poetry memorable. I call 'Rhyme and Rhythm' 'Rhythmic Remembrance'. Poems memorised go with one through life.

Change of Pace and Pitch: This gives colour, interest and is an aid to change of character.

Variety of Emphasis and Inflection: Convey meaning and emotion.

Change of Tone and Tune: Give variety of mood assisting the change of scene.

Attack: Make a strong attack on commencing a poem and always make a fresh attack at a new verse. This re-engages the interest of the audience.

Pause: Without pause, words would be meaningless. It must not be used at regular intervals, but at points of interest and to renew breath.

Verse Pause: A very short pause used at the end of each line of poetry to retain the rhythm, especially when speaking Lyric Verse.

Caesural Pause: A very important pause used at any place in a line of poetry to give the meaning.

Suspensory Pause: An important pause. It occurs at the end of a line in Lyric Verse where the meaning runs on to the following line. It is achieved by making a tiny pause at the end of a line, the voice remains at the same pitch, and the accent is placed on the second syllable of the first word in the next line thus retaining the sense without breaking the rhythm. *'Or like the rainbow's lovely form - S - Evanishing amid the storm'*.

Breath Control: Breath is the vehicle of speech. You speak on breath not with it. One must not attempt to obtain emotion by breathy speech. To take a deep breath through the nose before attempting to speak settles the nerves, thereafter breath is renewed through the mouth, thus ensuring an adequate supply of breath to carry the speech to the end of phrases and poetic lines. It is a carry-through process based on the Intercostal Diaphragmatic method, supported by the abdominal muscles which control the outgoing flow of air or phrase. Do not allow the tone to drop at line heads but final lines should carry a falling cadence.

Imagery: An important content in verse practised by the classical poets but not used to any great extent by the more practical modern poet. It is the translation of everyday speech into an image which on reading can be "Words that are windows to external things"; e.g. Burns did not say 'I turned up a wheen daises the day'. He said

> *'Wee modest crimson-tipped flow'r*
> *Thou'st met me in an evil hour*
> *For I maun crush amang the stour*
> *Thy slender stem'.*

Do not attempt to Anglicise Scots words or change Scots into English. Speak the poems as Burns wrote them. He never used an English word if he thought a Scots one more suitable. Always remember he was a perfect artist.

These basic elements complemented with good voice production and projection, clear articulation (consonants), enunciation (vowels) remembering that consonants are the frameworks, vowels the music of speech; will produce the well modulated voice, easily heard, pleasant and tuneful.

Irving Miller
FTCL, FLCM, LGSM, LTCL (Eloc)

CONTENTS

Up in the Morning Early

CHORUS
Up in the morning's no for me,
  Up in the morning early!
When a' the hills are cover'd wi snaw
  I'm sure it's winter fairly!

Cauld blaws the wind frae east to west,
  The drift is driving sairly,   sorely
Sae loud and shrill's I hear the blast –
  I'm sure it's winter fairly!

The birds sit chittering in the thorn,
  A day they fare but sparely;
And lang's the night frae e'en to morn –   evening
  I'm sure it's winter fairly

The words of this poem carefully emphasised will convey the chill of a cold morning.

My Wife's a Winsome Wee Thing

CHORUS
She is a winsome wee thing,
She is a handsome wee thing,
She is a lo'esome wee thing,
        This sweet wife o mine!

I never saw a fairer,
I never lo'ed a dearer,
And neist my heart I'll wear her,   next
For fear my jewel tine.   lose

The warld's wrack we share o't;   wreckage
The warstle and the care o't,   struggle
Wi her I'll blythely bear it,
And think my lot divine.

There is a pleasant lilt in this wee poem; try to convey it in word and tune.

Wee Willie Gray

Wee Willie Gray an his leather wallet,
Peel a willow-wand to be him boots and jacket!
The rose upon the brier will be him
    trouse an doublet –
The rose upon the brier will be him
    trouse and doublet!

Wee Willie Gray an his leather wallet,
Twice a lily-flower will be him sark and gravat!
Feathers of a flie wad feather up his bonnet –
Feathers of a flie wad feather up his bonnet!

A wee nursery rhyme to learn by heart.

The Highland Balou

Hee balou, my sweet wee Donald,	lullaby
Picture o the great Clanronald!	
Brawlie kens our wanton Chief	Finely knows
Wha gat my young Highland thief.	
Leeze me on thy bonie craigie!	Blessings, throat
An thou live, thou'll steal a naigie,	horse
Travel the country thro and thro,	
And bring hame a Carlisle cow!	
Thro the Lawlands, o'er the Border,	
Weel, my babie, may thou furder,	further
Herry the louns o the laigh Countrie	Harry, fools, low
Syne to the Highlands hame to me!	

This is a Lullaby and needs a gentle tone and tune, to lull a baby to sleep.

The Dusty Miller

Hey, the dusty miller,
  And his dusty coat!
He will win a shilling,
  Or he spend a groat!   Before
Dusty was the coat,
  Dusty was the colour,
Dusty was the kiss
  That I gat frae the miller!

Hey the dusty miller,
  And his dusty sack!
Leeze me on the calling   Blessings
  Fills the dusty peck!
Fills the dusty peck,
  Brings the dusty siller!
I wad gae my coatie
  For the dusty miller!

There is a rhythm here that gives the carefree life of a 'Jolly Miller'.

The Gard'ner wi his Paidle

When rosy May comes in wi flowers,
To deck her gay, green-spreading bowers,
Then busy, busy are his hours,
    The gard'ner wi his paidle.   spade

The crystal waters gently fa',
The merry birds are lovers a',
The scented breezes round him blaw –
    The gard'ner wi his paidle.

When purple morning starts the hare
To steal upon her early fare,
Then thro the dew he maun repair –   must
    The gard'ner wi his paidle.

When day, expiring in the west,
The curtain draws o Nature's rest,
He flies to her arms he loe's best,
    The gard'ner wi his paidle.

There is a description here of the long hours a gardener works;
Don't be doleful, use a bright happy mood.

The Ploughman

CHORUS
Then up wi't a', my Ploughman lad,
And hey, my merry Ploughman;
Of a' the trades that I do ken,
Commend me to the Ploughman.

The Ploughman he's a bony lad,
  His mind is ever true, jo,   darling
His garters knit below his knee,
  His bonnet it is blue, jo.

My Ploughman he comes hame at e'en
  He's aften wat and weary: often wet
Cast off the wat, put on the dry,
  And gae to bed, my Dearie.

I will wash my Ploughman's hose,
  And I will dress his o'erlay;   cravat
I will mak my Ploughman's bed,
  And cheer him late and early.

I hae been east, I hae been west,
  I hae been at Saint Johnston,
The boniest sight that e'er I saw
  Was th' Ploughman laddie dancin.

Snaw white stockins on his legs,
  And siller buckles glancin;
A gude blue bonnet on his head,
  And O but he was handsome!

Commend me to the Barn yard,
  And the Corn-mou, man;
I never gat my Coggie fou
  Till I met wi the Ploughman.

A good dancing rhythm here.

Out Over the Forth

Out over the Forth, I look to the north –
   But what is the north, and its Highlands to me?
The south nor the east gie ease to my breast,
   The far foreign land, or the wide rolling sea!

But I look to the west, when I gae to rest,
   That happy my dreams and my slumbers may be;
For far in the west lives he I loe best,
   The man that is dear to my babie and me.

This poem has an easy rhyme. All the words are standard English except "gie".

The Cardin O't, the Spinnin O't

CHORUS
The cardin o't, the spinnin o't,
   The warpin o't, the winnin o't!
When ilka ell cost me a groat,   each yard, fourpence
The tailor staw the lynin o't.

I coft a stane o haslock woo,   bought the soft wool from
   To make a wab to Johnie o't,   the lamb's neck, web
For Johnie is my only jo –   darling
   I lo'e him best of onie yet!

For tho his locks be lyart gray,   withered
   And tho his brow be beld aboon,   bald above
Yet I hae seen him on a day
   The pride of a' the parishen.   whole parish

The rhythm is easy to hold, the words 'go' with the spinning.
Every stage of spinning to the finished plaid is noted.

My Hoggie

What will I do gin my hoggie die?	should, lamb
My joy, my pride, my hoggie!	
My only beast, I had nae mae,	no more
And vow but I was vogie!	vain
The lee-lang night we watched the fauld,	live-long, fold
Me and my faithfu doggie;	
We heard nocht but the roaring linn,	waterfall
Amang the braes sae scroggie.	slopes, scrubby

But the houlet cry'd frae the castle wa',	owl
The blitter frae the boggie,	snipe
The tod reply'd upon the hill:	fox
I trembled for my hoggie.	
When day did daw, and cocks did craw,	
The morning it was foggie,	
An unco tyke lap o'er the dyke,	strange dog, fence
And maist has kill'd my hoggie!	almost

A much-loved pet lamb. A serious note must be used here. Anxiety is the mood.

I Dream'd I Lay

I dream'd I lay where flowers were springing	
Gaily in the sunny beam,	
List'ning to the wild birds singing,	
By a falling crystal stream;	
Straight the sky grew black and daring,	
Thro the woods the whirlwinds rave,	
Trees with aged arms were warring	
O'er the swelling, drumlie wave.	turbid

Such was my life's deceitful morning,	
Such the pleasures I enjoy'd!	
But lang or noon, loud tempests storming,	ere
A' my flowery bliss destroy'd.	
Tho fickle Fortune has deceiv'd me	
(She promis'd fair, and perform'd but ill),	
Of monie a joy and hope bereav'd me,	many
I bear a heart shall support me still.	

When reciting the poem 'Set a stoot hert to a stey brae'.

Epigram at Roslin Inn

My blessings on ye, honest wife!
I ne'er was here before;
Ye've wealth o gear for spoon and knife:
    Heart could not wish for more.
Heav'n keep you clear o sturt and strife,   trouble
    Till far ayont fourscore,   beyond
And by the Lord o death and life,
    I'll ne'er gae by your door!

A rhyming 'thank you' should be spoken with a happy thankful mood.

Mally's Meek, Mally's Sweet

CHORUS
Mally's meek, Mally's sweet,
   Mally's modest and discreet,
Mally's rare, Mally's fair,
   Mally's ev'ry way complete.

As I was walking up the street,
   A barefit maid I chanc'd to meet;
But O, the road was very hard
   For that fair maiden's tender feet!

It were mair meet that those fine feet
   Were weel laced up in silken shoon!
An 'twere more fit that she should sit
   Within yon chariot gilt aboon!

Her yellow hair, beyond compare,
   Comes tumbling down her swan-like neck,
And her twa eyes, like stars in skies,
   Would keep a sinking ship frae wreck!

This poem is like a fairy tale. When speaking it, think of Cinderella, her little feet and her golden chariot.

18

Fairest Maid on Devon Banks

CHORUS
Fairest maid on Devon banks,
  Crystal Devon, winding Devon,
Wilt thou lay that frown aside,
  And smile as thou wert wont to do?

Full well thou know'st I love thee dear –
Couldst thou to malice lend an ear!
O, did not Love exclaim:– 'Forbear,
  Nor use a faithful lover so!'

Then come, thou fairest of the fair,
Those wonted smiles, O, let me share,
And by thy beauteous self I swear
  No love but thine my heart shall know!

These lines were the last composed by the great National Bard of Scotland.

The Gallant Weaver

Where Cart rins rowin to the sea   runs
By monie a flower and spreading tree,
There lives a lad, the lad for men –
  He is a gallant weaver!
O, I had wooers aught or nine,   eight
They gied me rings and ribbons fine,
And I was fear'd my heart wad tine,   would be lost
  And I gied it to the weaver.

My daddie sign'd my tocher-band   marriage settlement
To gie the lad that has the land,
But to my heart I'll add my hand,
  And give it to the weaver.
While birds rejoice in leafy bowers,
While bees delight in opening flowers,
While corn grows green in summer showers,
  I love my gallant weaver.

Treat this poem with a pleasant tone and tune giving a good final cadence to the last line.

Rantin, Rovin Robin

This is a birthday poem.
Let it have a real bright couthy tone.
The lad is Robert Burns.

CHORUS
Robin was a rovin boy,
  Rantin, rovin, rantin, rovin,
Robin was a rovin boy,
  Rantin, rovin Robin!

There was a lad was born in Kyle,   at Alloway
But whatna day o whatna style,
I doubt it's hardly worth the while
  To be sae nice wi Robin.

Our monarch's hindmost year but ane   1759
Was five-and-twenty days begun,
'Twas then a blast on Janwar win'
  Blew hansel in on Robin.

The gossip keekit in his loof,   peered, face
Quo scho:– 'Wha lives will see the proof,
This waly boy will be nae coof: sturdy, fool
  I think we'll ca' him Robin.'

'He'll hae missfortunes great an sma
But ay a heart aboon them a'.
He'll be a credit till us a':
  We'll a' be proud o Robin!'

'But sure as three times three mak nine,
I see by ilka score and line,   every
This chap will dearly like our kin',
  So leeze me on thee, Robin!'   commend

20

Highland Laddie

She
The bonniest lad that e'er I saw,
  Bonie laddie, highland laddie,
Wore a plaid and was fu braw,
  Bonie Highland laddie.

On his head a bonnet blue,
  Bonie laddie, highland laddie,
His royal heart was firm and true,
  Bonie Highland laddie.

He
Trumpets sound and cannons roar,
  Bonie lassie, Lawland lassie,
And a' the hills wi echoes roar,
  Bonie Lawland lassie

Glory, Honor now invite
  Bonie lassie, Lawland lassie,
For freedom and my King to fight
  Bonie Lawland lassie.

She
The sun a backward course shall take,
  Bonie laddie, highland laddie,
Ere ought thy manly courage shake;
  Bonie Highland laddie.

Go, for yourself procure renown,
  Bonie laddie, highland laddie,
And for your lawful king his crown,
  Bonie highland laddie.

The contrasting verses here make a short dramatic piece by two speakers. Narrative.

O, This Is No My Ain Lassie

O, this is no my ain lassie,
 Fair tho the lassie be:
Weel ken I my ain lassie –
 Kind love is in her e'e.

I see a form, I see a face,
Ye weel may wi the fairest place:
It wants to me the witching grace,
 The kind of love that's in her e'e.

She's bonie, blooming, straight, and tall,
And lang has had my heart in thrall;
And ay it charms my very saul,
 The kind love that's in her e'e.

A thief sae pawkie is my Jean,   sly
To steal a blink by a' unseen!   glance
But gleg as light are lover's een,   bright
 When kind love is in the e'e.

It may escape the courtly sparks,
It may escape the learned clerks;
But well the watching lover marks
 The kind love that's in her e'e.

Give a pleasant lilting rhythm to this poem. Lyric.

Highland Harry Back Again

This is a little gem giving a fresh attack on each verse.

CHORUS
O, for him back again!
O, for him back again!
I wad gie a' Knockhaspie's land
For Highland Harry back again.

My Harry was a gallant gay,
 Fu stately strade he on the plain,   strode
But now he's banish'd far away:
 I'll never see him back again.

When a' the lave gae to their bed,   rest
 I wander dowie up the glen,   sadly
I set me down and greet my fill,   cry
 And ay I wish him back again.

O, were some villains hangit high,
 And ilka body had their ain,   every
Then I might see the joyfu sight,
 My Highland Harry back again!

Saw Ye Bonie Lesley

O, saw ye bonie Lesley,
  As she gaed o'er the Border?
She's gane, like Alexander,
  To spread her conquests farther!

To see her is to love her,
  And love but her for ever;
For nature made her what she is,
  And never made anither!

Thou art a queen, fair Lesley –
  Thy subjects, we before thee!
Thou art divine, fair Lesley –
  The hearts o men adore thee.

The Deil he could na skaith thee,   not harm
  Or aught that wad belang thee;
He'd look into thy bonie face,
  And say:– 'I canna wrang thee!'

The Powers aboon will tent thee,
  Misfortune sha'na steer thee:
Thou'rt like themsel sae lovely,
  That ill they'll ne'er let near thee.

Return again fair Lesley,
  Return to Caledonie!
That we may brag we hae a lass
  There's nane again sae bonie.

Contrast the first two verses with those that follow. 1 and 2 are descriptive, 3, 4 and 5 are addressed to Lesley.

The Weary Pund o Tow

CHORUS
The weary pund, the weary pund,   dressed flax fibre
  The weary pund o tow!
I think my wife will end her life
  Before she spin her tow.   flax fibre for spinning

I bought my wife a stane o lint   stone (14lbs)
  As guid as e'er did grow,
And a' that she has made o that
  Is ae puir pund o tow.   one

There sat a bottle in a bole   hole
  Beyont the ingle low;
And ay she took the tither souk   suck
  To drouk the stourie tow.   drench, dusty

Quoth I:– 'For shame, ye dirty dame,
  Gae spin your tap o tow!'
She took the rock, and wi a knock,   distaff
  She brake it o'er my pow.   pate

At last her feet – I sang to see't! –
  Gaed foremost o'er the knowe,   Went, knoll
And or I wad anither jad,   ere, wed, jade
  I'll wallop in a tow.

A worried man, a foolish wife – a humorous narrative must be given here.

The Wounded Hare

Inhuman man! curse on thy barb'rous art,
  And blasted by thy murder-aiming eye;
    May never pity soothe thee with a sigh,
Nor never pleasure glad thy cruel heart!

Go live, poor wanderer of the wood and field,
  The bitter little of life that remains!
    No more the thickening brakes and verdant plains
to thee shall home, or food, or pastime yield.

Seek, mangled wretch, some place of wonted rest,
  No more of rest, but now thy dying bed!
    The sheltering rushes whistling o'er thy head,
The cold earth with thy bloody bosom prest.

Oft as by winding Nith I, musing, wait
  The sober eve, or hail the cheerful dawn,
    I'll miss thee sporting o'er the dewy lawn,
And curse the ruffian's aim, and mourn thy hapless fate.

Speak this poem in defence of all suffering animals.

24

O, Kenmure's On and Awa, Willie

O, Kenmure's on and awa, Willie,
  O, Kenmure's on and awa!
An Kenmure's lord's the bravest lord
  That ever Galloway saw!
Success to Kenmure's band, Willie,
  Success to Kenmure's band!
There's no a heart that fears a Whig
  That rides by Kenmure's hand.

Here's Kenmure's health in wine, Willie,
  Here's Kenmure's health in wine!
There's ne'er a coward o Kenmure's blude,
  Nor yet o Gordon's line.
O, Kenmure's lads are men, Willie,
  O, Kenmure's lads are men!
Their hearts and swords are metal true,
  And that their faes shall ken.   *foes*

The'll live or die wi fame, Willie,
  They'll live or die wi fame!
But soon wi sounding Victorie
  May Kenmure's lord come hame!
Here's him that's far awa, Willie,
  Here's him that's far awa!
And here's the flower that I lo'e best,
  The rose that's like the snaw!   *the Jacobite rose*

A bright martial poem. Kenmure Castle is on the banks of Loch Ken in bonnie Galloway.

The Banks of the Devon

How pleasant the banks of the clear winding Devon,
　With green spreading bushes and flow'rs blooming fair!
But the boniest flow're on the banks of the Devon
　Was once a sweet bud on the braes of the Ayr.

Mild be the sun on this sweet blushing flower,
　In the gay rosy morn, as it bathes in the dew!
And gentle the fall of the soft vernal shower,
　That steals on the evening each leaf to renew!

O, spare the dear blossom, ye orient breezes,
　With chill, hoary wing as ye usher the dawn!
And far be thou distant, thou reptile that seizes
　The verdure and pride of the garden or lawn!

Let Bourbon exult in his gay gilded lilies,
　And England triumphant display her proud rose!
A fairer than either adorns the green vallies,
　Where Devon, sweet Devon, meandering flows.

Let this poem move along as smoothly as the clear winding stream.

The Night Was Still

The night was still, and o'er the hill
　the moon shone on the castle wa',
The mavis sang, while dew-drops hang
　Around her on the castle wa':

Sae merrily they danc'd the ring
　Frae eenin till the cock did craw,
And ay the o'erword o the spring
　Was:– 'Irvine's bairns are bonie a'!'

evening

children

Another wee rhyme; convey the mood of the happy bairns.

On Scaring Some Water-Foul in Loch Turit

This poem is descriptive. The words describe the
fellow-feeling of the poet for all things in nature.

Why, ye tenants of the lake,
For me your wat'ry haunt forsake?
Tell me, fellow-creatures, why
At my presence thus you fly?
Why disturb your social joys,
Parent, filial, kindred ties? –
Common friend to you and me,
Nature's gifts to all are free:
Peaceful keep your dimpling wave,
Busy feed, or wanton lave;
Or, beneath the sheltering rock,
Bide the surging billow's shock.

Conscious, blushing for our race,
Soon, too soon your fears I trace.
Man, your proud, usurping foe,
Would be lord of all below:
Plumes himself in freedom's pride,
Tyrant stern to all beside.

The eagle, from the cliffy brow,
Marking you his prey below,
In his breast no pity dwells,
Strong necessity compels:
But Man, to whom alone is giv'n
A ray direct from pitying Heav'n,
Glories in his heart humane –
And creatures for his pleasure slain!

In these savage, liquid plains,
Only known to wand'ring swains,
Where the mossy riv'let strays
Far from human haunts and ways,
All on Nature you depend,
And life's poor season peaceful spend.

Or, of Man's superior might
Dare invade your native right,
On the lofty ether borne,
Man with all his powers you scorn;
Swiftly seek, on clanging wings,
Other lakes, and other springs;
And the foe you cannot brave,
Scorn at least to be his slave.

There'll Never be Peace Till Jamie Comes Hame

By yon castle wa' at the close of the day,
I heard a man sing, tho his head it was grey,
And as he was singing, the tears doon came, –
'There'll never be peace till Jamie comes hame!'

'The Church is in ruins, the State is in jars,
Delusion, oppressions, and murderous wars,
We dare na weel say't, but we ken wha's to blame –
There'll never be peace till Jamie comes hame!

'My seven braw sons for Jamie drew sword,
But now I greet round their green beds in the yerd;
It brak the sweet heart o my faithu auld dame –
There'll never be peace till Jamie comes hame!

'Now life is a burden that bows me down,
Sin I tint my bairns, and he tint his crown;
But till my last moments my words are the same –
There'll never be peace till Jamie comes hame!'

This poem refers to the exiled Stuart king. Fill your voice with longing.

The Banks of Nith

There is a fine flowing poem –
endeavour to give it rhythm.

The Thames flows proudly to the sea,
    Where royal cities stately stand;
But sweeter flows the Nith to me,
    Where Cummins ance had high command. the Red Comyn
When shall I see that honor'd land,
    That winding stream I love so dear?
Must wayward Fortune's adverse hand
    For ever – ever keep me here?

How lovely, Nith, thy fruitful vales,
    Where bounding hawthorns gayly bloom,
And sweetly spread thy sloping dales,
    Where lambkins wanton thro the broom!
Tho wandering now must be my doom,
    Far from thy bonie banks and braes,
May there my latest hours consume,
    Amang my friends of early days!

Dainty Davie

CHORUS
Meet me on the Warlock Knowe,   wizard knoll
   Dainty Davie, Dainty Davie!
There I'll spend the day wi you,
   My ain dear Dainty Davie.   own

Now rosy May comes in wi flowers
To deck her gay, green-spreading bowers;
And now comes in the happy hours
   To wander wi my Davie.

The crystal waters round us fa'
The merry birds are lovers a',
The scented breezes round us blaw
   A wandering wi my Davie.

When purple morning starts the hare
To steal upon her early fare,
Then thro the dews I will repair
   To meet my faithfu Davie.

When day, expiring in the west,
The curtain draws o Nature's rest,
I flee to his arms I loe the best:
   And that's my ain dear Davie!

Indeed a dainty poem, so descriptive
of morning and evening.

The Belles of Mauchline

In Mauchline there dwells six proper young belles,
   The pride of the place and its neighbourhood a',
Their carriage and dress, a stranger would guess,
   In Lon'on or Paris, they'd gotten it a'.

Miss Miller is fine, Miss Markland's divine,
   Miss Smith she has wit, and Miss Betty is braw,
There's beauty and fortune to get wi Miss Morton;
   But Armour's the jewel for me o them a'.

A short poem with much variety of modulation.

Blythe Was She

Blythe, blythe and merry was she,
Blythe was she butt and ben,
Blythe by the banks of Earn,
And blythe in Glenturit glen!

By Oughtertyre grows the aik,   oak
  On Yarrow banks the birken shaw;   birch, wood
But Phemie was a bonier lass
  Than braes o Yarrow ever saw.   slopes

Her looks were like a flow'r in May,
  Her smile was like a simmer morn:
She tripped by the banks o Earn,
  As light's a bird upon a thorn.

Her bonie face it was as meek,
  As onie lamb upon a lea.
The evening sun was ne'er sae sweet
  As was the blink o Phemie's e'e.   glance

The Highland hills I've wander'd wide,
  As o'er the Lawlands I hae been,
But Phemie was the blythest lass
  That ever trod the dewy green.

A straight forward poem of praise which
requires a firm attack and tune.

My Heart's in the Highlands

CHORUS
My heart's in the Highlands, my heart is not here
My heart's in the Highlands, a-chasing the deer,
A-chasing the wild deer, and following the roe –
My heart's in the Highlands, wherever I go!

Farewell to the Highlands, farewell to the North,
The birthplace of valour, the country of worth!
Wherever I wander, wherever I rove,
The hills of the Highlands for ever I love.

Farwell to the mountains, high-cover'd with snow,
Farwell to the straths and green valleys below,
Farwell to the forests and wild-hanging woods,
Farwell to the torrents and loud-pouring floods!

During his Highland tour Burns wrote many poems describing
the scenery. This is one which has a real melody.

Amang the Trees

Amang the trees, where humming bees
  At buds and flowers were hinging, O,
Auld Caledon drew out her drone,
  And to her pipe was singing, O.
'Twas Pibroch, Sang, Strathspeys and Reels –
  She dirl'd them aff fu clearly, O,   rang
When there cam a yell o foreign squeels,
  That dang her tapsalteerie, O!   knocked upside down

Their capon craws an queer 'ha, ha's,'
  They made our lugs grow eerie, O.   ears
The hungry bike did scrape and fyke,   swarm, make a fuss
  Till we were wae and weary, O.   sad
But a royalist ghaist, wha ance was cas'd   King James I (1394-1437) imprisoned in England, 1406-24
  A prisoner, aughteen year awa,
He fir'd a Fiddler in the North,
  That dang them tapsalteerie, O!

This song was dedicated to a famous 18th century fiddler, Neil Gow.

I'm O'er Young to Marry Yet

CHORUS
I'm o'er young, I'm o'er young,
  I'm o'er young to marry yet!
I'm o'er young, 'twad be a sin
  To tak me frae my mammie yet.

I am my mammie's ae bairn,   only child
  Wi unco folk I weary, Sir;   strangers
And lying in a strange bed,
  I'm fley'd it make me eerie, Sir.   afraid

Hallowmass is come and gane,
  The nights are lang in winter, Sir,
And you and I in ae bed,   one
  In trowth, I dare na venture, Sir!   truth

There is a shyness here that must be shown in
the mood of the speaker.

Fu loud and shrill the frosty wind
  Blaws thro the leafless timmer, Sir;   woods
But if ye come this gate again,   way
  I'll aulder be gin simmer, Sir.   older be by

A Rose-Bud by My Early Walk

A rose-bud, by my early walk
Adown a corn-inclosed bawk,   footpath
Sae gently bent its thorny stalk,
    All on a dewy morning.
Ere twice the shades o dawn are fled,
In a' its crimson glory spread,
And drooping rich the dewy head,
    It scents the early morning.

With the bush her covert nest
A little linnet fondly prest,
The dew sat chilly on her breast,
    Sae early in the morning.
She soon shall see her tender brood,
The pride, the pleasure o the wood,
Amang the fresh green leaves bedew'd,
    Awauk the early morning.   awake

So thou, dear bird, young Jeany fair,
On trembling string or vocal air,
Shall sweetly pay the tender care
    That tents thy early morning!   guards
So thou, sweet rose-bud, young and gay,
Shall beauteous blaze upon the day,
And bless the parent's evening ray
    That watch'd thy early morning!

This poem was written about wee Jean Cruikshank. Speak it as if you see her as a rosebud. Narrative lyric.

Now Spring Has Clad the Grove in Green

Now spring has clad the grove in green,
   And strew'd the lea wi flowers;
The furrow'd, waving corn is seen
   Rejoice in fostering showers;

The trout within yon wimpling burn   meandering brook
   Glides swift, a silver dart,
And, safe beneath the shady thorn,
   Defies the angler's art:

The little floweret's peaceful lot,
   In yonder cliff that grows,
Which, save the linnet's flight, I wot,
   Nae ruder visit knows.

The waken'd lav'rock warbling springs,   lark
   And climbs the early sky,
Winnowing blythe his dewy wings
   In Morning's rosy eye:

In this poem, the words need a caressing touch to give the joy of Spring.

The Jolly Beggars – A Cantata

A pigmy scraper on a fiddle,
Wha us'd to trystes an fairs to driddle,   *cattle round-ups, dawdle*
Her strappin limb an gawsie middle   *buxom*
      (He reach'd nae higher)
Had hol'd his heartie like a riddle,
      An blawn't on fire.   *blown it*

Wi hand on hainch and upward e'e,   *haunch*
He croon'd his gamut, one, two, three
Then in an *arioso* key,
      The wee Apollo
Set off wi *allegretto* glee
      His *giga* solo:–

I am a fiddler to my trade,
An a' the tunes that e'er I play'd
The sweetest still to wife or maid,
   Was 'Whistle owre the lave o't.'

Let me ryke up to dight that tear,   *reach, wipe*
An go wi me an be my dear;
And then your every care an fear
   May whistle owre the lave o't.

At kirns an weddins we'se be there,   *harvest-homes*
An O, sae nicely's we will fare!
We'll bowse about till Daddie Care
   Sing *Whistle owre the lave o't.*

Sae merrily the banes we'll pyke,   *bones, pick*
An sun oursels about the dyke;   *fence*
An at our leisure, when ye like,
   We'll – whistle owre the lave o't!

But bless me wi your heav'n o charms,
An while I kittle hair on thairms,   *tickle, catguts*
Hunger, cauld, an a' sick harms,
   May whistle owre the lave o't.

This poem needs all the gay humour you can give. A jolly wee fiddler.
Pause between verses 2 & 3, to change over to the fiddler speaking. Narrative by the fiddler.

O, That I Had Ne'er Been Married

CHORUS

Ance crowdie, twice crowdie,   gruel
* Three times crowdie in a day!*
Gin ye crowdie onie mair,   If, any more
* Ye'll crowdie a' my meal away.*

O, that I had ne'er been married,
  I wad never had nae care!
Now I've gotten wife and bairns,   children
  An they cry 'Crowdie' ever mair.

Waefu Want and Hunger fley me,   Woeful, thrash
  Glowrin by the hallan en';   Staring, porch-end
Sair I fech them at the door,   Sore, fight
  But ay I'm eerie they come ben.   afraid, inside

Try to give the mood of a weary father sighing about feeding his bairns when it is difficult to make ends meet.
The tone has to be an anxious one.

Robin Shure in Hairst

Here we have Burns having a joke at his lawyer-friend, Robert Ainslie. Endeavour to give the sarcastic note on the last lines. Lyric.

CHORUS

Robin shure in hairst,   reaped, harvest
* I shure wi him:*
Fient a heuk had I,   not a sickle
* Yet I stack by him.*   stuck

I gaed up to Dunse,   went
  To warp a wab o plaiden, weave, web, tweed
At his daddie's yett,   gate
  Wha met me but Robin!

Was na Robin bauld,   bold
  Tho I was a cotter?
Play'd me sick a trick,
  An me the Eller's dochter! Elder's daughter

Robin promis'd me
  A' my winter vittle: food
Fient haet he had but three Devil have it (i.e. nothing)
  Guse-feathers and a whittle! goose-quills, knife

35

Address to the Toothache

My curse upon your venom'd stang,   *sting*
That shoots my tortur'd gums alang,
An thro my lug gies monie a twang   *ear, twinge*
    Wi gnawing vengeance,
Tearing my nerves wi bitter pang,
    Like racking engines!

A' down my beard the slavers trickle,   *saliva*
I throw the wee stools o'er the mickle,
While round the fire the giglets keckle,   *cackle*
    To see me loup,   *dance*
An raving mad, I wish a heckle   *heckling-comb*
    Were i' their doup!   *backside*

When fevers burn, or ague freezes,
Rheumatics gnaw, or colic squeezes,
Our neebors sympathise to ease us,   *neighbours*
    Wi pitying moan;
But thee! – thou hell o a' diseases –
    They mock our groan!

Of a' the numerous human dools –   *woes*
Ill-hairsts, daft bargains, cutty-stools,   *harvest, mad*
Or worthy frien's laid i' the mools,   *crumbling earth*
    Sad sight to see!
The tricks o knaves, or fash o fools –   *annoyance*
    Thou bear'st the gree!   *takest the prize*

Whare'er that place be priests ca' Hell,
Whare a' the tones o misery yell,
An ranked plagues their numbers tell,
    In dreadfu raw,   *row*
Thou, Toothache, surely bear'st the bell,
    Amang them a'!

O thou grim, mischief-making chiel,   *fellow*
That gars the notes o discord squeel,   *makes*
Till human kind aft dance a reel
    In gore, a shoe-thick,
Gie a' the faes o Scotland's weal   *Give, foes*
    A towmond's toothache!   *twelve month's*

Have a feeling of pain in your words here and a good climax on the last lines. Narrative, the speaker is the poet.

Logan Braes

O Logan, sweetly didst thou glide
That day I was my Willie's bridge,
And years sin syne hae o'er us run   since then
Like Logan to the simmer sun.
But now thy flowery banks appear
Like drumlie winter, dark and drear,   muddy
While my dear lad maun face his faes   must, foe
Far, far frae me and logan braes.   hillsides

Again the merry month of May
Has made our hills and vallies gay;
The birds rejoice in leafy bowers,
The bees hum round the breathing flowers:
Blythe Morning lifts his rosy eye,
And Evening's tears are tears o joy:
My soul delightless a' surveys,
While Willie's far frae Logan braes.

Within yon milk-white hawthorn bush,
Amang her nestlings sits the thrush:
Her faithfu mate will share her toil,
Or wi his song her cares beguile.
But I wi my sweet nurslings here,
Nae mate to help, nae mate to cheer,
Pass widow'd nights and joyless days,
While Willie's far frae Logan braes.

O, wae be to you, Men o State,
That brethren rouse in deadly hate!
As ye make monie a fond heart mourn,
Sae may it on your heads return!
Ye mind na 'mid your cruel joys
The widow's tears, the orphan's cries,
But soon may peace bring happy days,
And Willie hame to Logan Braes!

A truly pastoral poem which by the use of rhythm, pause and emphasis will gain the atmosphere and hope. Lyric.

Meg o the Mill

O ken ye what Meg of the mill has gotten?
An ken ye what Meg o the mill has gotten?
She's gotten a coof wi a claute o siller,   *dolt, hoard, money*
And broken the heart o the barley miller!

The miller was strappin, the miller was ruddy,
A heart like a lord, and a hue like a lady.
The laird was a widdifu, bleerit knurl! –   *gallows-worthy, dwarf*
She's left the guid fellow, and taen the churl.

The miller, he hecht her a heart leal and loving;   *offered, loyal*
The laird did address her wi matter mair moving:
A fine pacing-horse wi a clear, chained bridle,
A whip by her side, and a bonie side-saddle!

O, wae on the siller – it is sae prevailing!   *woe*
And wae on the love that is fixed on a mailen!   *farm*
A tocher's nae word in a true lover's parl,   *dowry, speech*
But gie me my love, and a fig for the warl!

The message here is not of siller but of love. Bring that advice out when speaking the poem. Narrative.

My Luve is Like a Red, Red Rose

O' my luve is like a red, red rose,
  That's newly sprung in June.
O, my luve is like the melodie,
  That's sweetly play'd in tune.

As fair art thou, my bonie lass,
  So deep in luve am I,
And I will luve thee still my dear,
  Till a' the seas gang dry.

Till a' the seas gang dry, my dear,
  And the rocks melt wi the sun!
And I will luve thee still, my dear,
  While the sands o life shall run.

And fare thee weel, my only luve!
  And fare thee weel, a while!
And I will come again, my luve,
  Tho it were ten thousand mile!

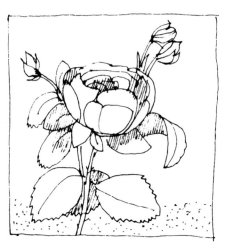

One of the finest love poems ever written.
Give it a sincere note of love and reverence. Lyric.

The Cotter's Saturday Night

November chill blaws loud wi angry sugh;   wail
    The short'ning winter-day is near a close;
The miry beasts retreating frae the pleugh;
    The black'ning trains o craws to their repose:
    The toil-worn Cotter frae his labor goes, –
This night his weekly moil is at an end,
    Collects his spades, his mattocks, and his hoes,
Hoping the morn in ease and rest to spend,
And weary, o'er the moor, his course does hameward bend.

At length his lonely cot appears in view,
    Beneath the shelter of an aged tree;
Th' expectant wee-things, toddlin, stacher through   stagger
    To meet their dad, wi flichterin noise and glee,   fluttering
    His wee bit ingle, blinkin bonilie,
His clean hearth-stane, his thrifty wifie's smile,
    The lisping infant, prattling at his knee,
Does a' his weary kiaugh and care beguile,   anxiety
And makes him quite forget his labor and his toil.

Belyve, the elder bairns come drapping in,   By and by
    At service out, amang the farmers roun;
Some ca' the pleugh, some herd, some tentie rin   drive, heedful run
    A cannie errand to a neebor town: neighbouring
    Their eldest hope, their Jenny, woman grown,
In youthfu bloom, love sparkling in her e'e,
    Comes hame; perhaps, to show a braw new gown,
Or deposits her said-won penny-fee,   hard-earned wages
To help her parents dear, if they in hardship be.

This is a long and much loved poem. Speak it as a narrative – that is as a story.

Epistle to a Young Friend

I lange hae thought, my youthfu friend,
  A something to have sent you,
Tho it should serve nae ither end
  Than just a kind memento:
But how the subject-theme may gang,
  Let time and chance determine:
Perhaps it may turn out a sang;
  Perhaps, turn out a sermon.

Ye'll try the world soon, my lad;
  And, Andrew dear, believe me,
Ye'll find mankind an unco squad,   strange
  And muckle they may grieve ye:
For care and trouble set your thought,
  Ev'n when your end's attained;
And a' your views may come to nought,
  Where ev'ry nerve is strained.

I'll no say, men are villains a':
  The real, harden'd wicked,
Wha hae nae check but human law,
  Are to a few restricked;
But, och! mankind are unco weak,   mighty
  An little to be trusted;
If *self* the wavering balance shake,
  It's rarely right adjusted!

Yet they wha fa' in Fortune's strife,
  Their fate we should na censure;
For still, th' important end of life
  They equally may answer:
A man may hae an honest heart,
  Tho poortith hourly stare him;   poverty
A man may tak a neebor's part,
  Yet hae nae cash to spare him.

Ay free, aff han', your story tell,
  When wi a bosom cronie;
But still keep something to yoursel
  Ye scarcely tell to onie:
Conceal yoursel as weel's ye can
  Frae critical dissection:
But keek thro ev'ry other man,   look
  Wi sharpen'd, sly inspection.

Epistle to a Young Friend

The sacred lowe o weel-plac'd love,   *flame*
   Luxuriantly indulge it;
But never tempt th' illict rove,
   Tho naething should divulge it:
I waive the quantum o the sin,
   The hazard of concealing;
But, och! it hardens a' within.
   And petrifies the feeling!

To catch Dame Fortune's golden smile,
   Assiduous wait upon her;
And gather gear by ev'ry wile
   That's justify'd by honor:
Not for to hide it in a hedge,
   Not for a train-attendant;
But for the glorious privilege
   Of being independent.

The fear o Hell's a hangman's whip
   To haud the wretch in order;
But where ye feel your honour grip,
   Let that ay be your border:
Its slightest touches, instant pause –
   Debar a' side-pretences;
And resolutely keep its laws,
   Uncaring consequences.

The great Creator to revere,
   Must sure become the creature;
But still the preaching cant forbear,
   An ev'n the rigid feature:
Yet ne'er with wits profane to range
   Be complaisance extended;
An atheist-laugh's a poor exchange
   For Deity offended!

When ranting round in Pleasure's ring,   *frolicking*
   Religion may be blinded;
Or if she gie a random sting,
   It may be little minded;
But when on Life we're tempest-driv'n –
   A conscience but a canker –
A correspondence fix'd wi' Heav'n,
   Is sure a noble anchor!

Adieu, dear, amiable youth!
   Your heart can ne'er be wanting!
May prudence, fortitude, and truth,
   Erect your brow undaunting!
In ploughman phrase, 'God send you speed,'
   Still daily to grow wiser;
And may ye better reck the rede,
   Than ever did th' adviser!

The finest thing about great poetry is that it is applicable to the present day. The words make it easy to project the thought. A narrative letter.

41

The Gloomy Night is Gath'ring Fast

The gloomy night is gath'ring fast,
Loud roars the wild inconstant blast;
Yon murky cloud is filled with rain,
I see it driving o'er the plain;
The hunter now has left the moor,
The scatt'red coveys meet secure;
While I here wander, prest with care,
Along the lonely banks of Ayr.

The Autumn mourns her rip'ning corn
By early Winter's ravage torn;
Across her placid, azure sky,
She sees the scowling tempest fly;
Chill runs my blood to hear it rave;
I think upon the stormy wave,
Where many a danger I must dare,
Far from the bonie banks of Ayr.

'Tis not the surging billows' roar,
'Tis not that fatal, deadly shore;
Tho death in ev'ry shape appear,
The wretched have no more to fear:
But round my heart the ties are bound,
The heart transpiec'd with many a wound;
These bleed afresh, those ties I tear,
To leave the bonie banks of Ayr.

Farewell, old Coila's hills and dales,
Her heathy moors and winding vales;
The scenes where wretched Fancy roves,
Pursuing past unhappy loves!
Farewell my friends! farewell my foes!
My peace with these, my love with those –
The bursting tears my heart declare,
Farewell, my bonie banks of Ayr!

The mood here is a sad one, but must not be monotonous. Lyric.

Wee Jenny to her graunie says,   Jenny Broun, the poet's cousin
  'Will you go wi me, graunie?
I'll eat the apple at the glass,
  I gat frae uncle Johnie':
She fuff't her pipe wi sic a lunt,   puffed, smoke
  In wrath she was sae vap'rin,
She notic't na an aizle brunt   burning ember
    Her braw, new, worset apron   worsted
      Out thro that night.

'Ye little skelpie-limmer's-face!   hussy
  I daur you try sic sportin,
As seek the Foul Thief onie place,   Devil
  For him to spae your fortune: tell
Nae doubt but ye may get a sight!
  Great cause ye hae to fear it;
For monie a ane has gotten a fright,
  An liv'd an died deleeret,
    On sic a night.

In the days of Robert Burns there were many ways of telling fortunes.
Here, wee Jenny wants to see in the looking glass who will be her sweetheart. Narrative.

The Cotter's Saturday Night

With joy unfeign'd, brothers and sisters meet,
    And each for other's welfare kindly spiers: *enquiries*
The social hours, swift-wing'd, unnotic'd fleet;
    Each tells the uncos that he sees or hears.
    The parents partial eye their hopeful years;
Anticipation forward points the view;
    The mother, wi her needle and her sheers   *scissors*
Gars auld claes look amaist as weel's the new;   *makes clothes almost*
The father mixes a' wi admonition due.

Their master's and their mistress's command,
    The younkers a' are warned to obey;   *youngsters*
And mind their labors wi an eydent hand,   *diligent*
And ne'er tho out o sight, to jauk or play;   *fool about*
    'And O! be sure to fear the Lord alway,
And mind your duty, duly, morn and night;
    Lest in temptation's path ye gang astray,
Implore His counsel and assisting might:
They never sought in vain that sought the Lord aright.'

But hark! a rap comes gently to the door;
    Jenny, wha kens the meaning o the same,
Tells how a neebor lad came o'er the moor,
    To do some errands, and convoy her hame.
    The wily mother sees the conscious flame
Sparkle in Jenny's e'e, and flush her cheek;
    With heart-struck anxious care, inquires his name,
Whil Jenny hafflins is afraid to speak;   *half*
Weel-pleas'd the mother hears, it's nae wild, worthless rake.

Wi kindly welcome, Jenny brings him ben;   *inside*
    A strappin youth, he takes the mother's eye;
Blythe Jenny sees the visit's no ill taen;
    The father cracks of horses, pleughs and kye.   *chats, castle*
    The youngster's artless heart o'erflows wi joy,
But blate an laithfu, scarce can weel behave;   *shy, sheepish*
    The mother, wi a woman's wiles, can spy
What makes the youth sae bashful and sae grave;
Weel-pleas'd to think her bairn's respected like the lave.   *child, rest*

A very descriptive poem of Scottish country life in Burns's day. Make the verses come alive. Narrative.

Sweet Afton

Flow gently, sweet Afton, among thy green braes   slopes
Flow gently, I'll sing thee a song in thy praise!
My Mary's asleep by thy murmuring stream –
Flow gently, sweet Afton, disturb not her dream!

Thou stock dove whose echo resounds thro the glen,
Ye wild whistling blackbirds in yon thorny den,
Thou green-crested lapwing, thy screaming forbear –
I charge you, disturb not my slumbering Fair.

How lofty, sweet Afton, thy neighbouring hills,
Far mark'd with the courses of clear, winding rills!
There daily I wander, as noon rises high,
My flocks and my Mary's sweet cot in my eye.

How pleasant thy banks and green vallies below,
Where wild in the woodlands the primroses blow
There oft, as mild Ev'ning weeps over the lea,
The sweet-scented birk shades my Mary and me.   birch

Thy crystal stream, Afton, how lovely it glides,
And winds by the cot where my Mary resides!   cottage
How wanton thy waters her snowy feet lave,   wash
As, gathering sweet flowerets, she stems thy clear wave!

Flow gently, sweet Afton, among thy green braes!
Flow gently, sweet river, the theme of my lays!
My Mary's asleep by thy murmuring stream –
Flow gently, sweet Afton, disturb not her dream!

This is a caressing poem – it must have a delicate touch. Lyric.

To a Louse

Ha! whare ye gaun' ye crowlin ferlie?   crawling marvel
Your impudence protects you sairly;   marvel
I canna say but ye strunt rarely   strut
     Owre gauze and lace,
Tho faith! I fear ye dine but sparely
     On sic a place.

I wad na been surpris'd to spy
You on an auld wife's flainen toy;   flannel cap
Or aiblins some bit duddie boy,   perhaps, small
     On's wyliecoat;   ragged vest
But Miss's fine Lunardi! fye!   balloon bonnet
     How daur ye do't?

O Jeany, dinna toss your head,
And set your beauties a' abread!   abroad
Ye little ken what cursed speed
     The blastie's makin!   pest
Thae winks an finger-ends, I dread,   Those
     Are notice takin!

O wad some Power the giftie gie us
To see oursels as ithers see us!
It wad frae monie a blunder free us,
     An foolish notion:
What airs in dress and gait wad lea'e us,
     An ev'n devotion!

Burns is a master of satire. The tone should be one of surprise at such a sight. Narrative, but lyric as the poet speaks.

Ca' the Yowes to the Knowes

CHORUS
Ca' the yowes to the knowes,   ewe, knolls
Ca' them where the heather grows,
Ca' them where the burnie rowes,   streamlet
 My bonie dearie.

Hark, the mavis e'ening sang   thrush
Sounding Clouden's woods amang
Then a-faulding let us gang,
 My bonie dearie.

We'll gae down by Clouden side,   go
Thro the hazels, spreading wide
O'er the waves that sweetly glide
 To the moon sae clearly.

Yonder Clouden's silent towers
Where, at moonshine's midnight hours,
O'er the dewy bending flowers
 Fairies dance sae cheery.

Ghaist nor bogle shalt thou fear –   Ghost, demon
Thou'rt to Love and Heav'n sae dear
Nocht of ill may come thee near,
 My bonie dearie.

The silent towers are the ruins of Lincluden Abbey, Dumfries. This poem can be treated as a gentle lullaby. The simple sweetness of this poem requires a simple delivery. Lyric.

To a Mountain Daisy

Wee, modest, crimson-tipped flow'r,
Thou's met me in an evil hour;
For I maun crush amang the stoure   dust
        Thy slender stem:
To spare thee now is past my pow'r,
        Thou bonie gem.

Alas! it's no thy neebor sweet,
The bonie lark companion meet,
Bending thee 'mang the dewy weet,   wet
        Wi speckl'd breast!
When upward-springing, blythe, to greet
        The purpling east.

Cauld blew the bitter-biting north
Upon thy early, humble birth;
Yet cheerfuly thou glinted forth   shone
        Amid the storm,
Scarce rear'd above the parent-earth
        Thy tender form.

The flaunting flow'rs our gardens yield,
High shelt'ring woods and wa's maun shield;   must
But thou, beneath the random bield   shelter
        O clod or stane,
Adorns the histie stibble-field,   bare
        Unseen, alane.

There, in thy scanty mantle clad,
Thy snawie bosom sun-ward spread,
Thou lifts thy unassuming head
        In humble guise;
But now the share uptears thy bed,
        And low thou lies!

Here Burns speaks with simplicity and sincerity. Give the words these qualities. Lyric.

Does Haughty Gaul Invasion Threat?

Does haughty Gaul invasion threat?
    Then let the loons beware Sir!   *fools*
There's wooden walls upon our seas
    And volunteers on shore, Sir!
The Nith shall run to Corsincon,
    And Criffel sink in Solway,
Ere we permit a foreign foe
    On British ground to rally!

O, let us not, like snarling tykes,   *dogs*
    In wrangling be divided,
Till, slap! come in an unco loon,   *uncommon*
    And wi a rung decide it!   *cudgel*
Be Britain still to Britain true,
    Amang ourselves united!
For never but by British hands
    Maun British wrangs be righted!   *Must*

The kettle o the Kirk and State,
    Perhaps a clout may fail in't;   *patch*
But Deil a foreign tinkler loon
    Shall ever ca' a nail in't!
Our fathers' blude the kettle bought,
    And wha wad dare to spoil it,
By Heav'ns! the sacrilegious dog
    Shall fuel be to boil it!

The wretch that would a tyrant own,
    And the wretch, his true-sworn brother,
Who would set the mob above the throne,
    May they be damn'd together!
Who will not sing *God Save the King*
    Shall hang as high's the steeple;
But while we sing *God Save the King*,
    We'll ne'er forget the people!

A really patriotic poem. Give it a loud clear voice. Narrative.

Duncan Gray

Duncan Gray cam here to woo
    (Ha, ha, the wooing o't!)
On blythe Yule-night when we were fou   drunk
    (Ha, ha, the wooing o't).
Maggie coost her head fu high,   tossed
Look'd asklent and unco skeigh,   disdainfully, very skittish
Gart poor Duncan stand abeigh,   Made, off
    Ha, ha, the wooing o't!

Duncan fleech'd, and Duncan pray'd: wheedled
    (Ha, ha, the wooing o't!)
Meg was deaf as Ailsa Craig,
    (Ha, ha, the wooing o't!),
Duncan sigh'd baith out and in,   both
Grat his e'en baith blear't an blin',   Wept, blurred
Spak o lowpin o'er a linn –
    Ha, ha, the wooing o't!

Time and Chance are but a tide
    (Ha, ha, the wooing o't!):
Slighted love is sair to bide
    (Ha, ha, the wooing o't!).
'Shall I like a fool,' quoth he,
'For a haughty hizzie die?   hussy
She may go to – France for me!'
    Ha, ha, the wooing o't!

How it comes, let doctors tell,
    (Ha, ha, the wooing o't):
Meg grew sick, as he grew hale,   healthy
    (Ha, ha, the wooing o't).
Something in her bosom wrings,
For relief a sigh she brings,
And O! her een they spak sic things! –   eyes
    Ha, ha, the wooing o't!

Duncan was a lad o grace
    (Ha, ha, the wooing o't),
Maggie's was a piteous case,
    (Ha, ha, the wooing o't!):
Duncan could na be her death,
Swelling pity smoor'd his wrath;   smothered
Now they're crouse and canty baith –   proud, jolly
    Ha, ha, the wooing o't!

There is much humour here. Endeavour to project it – the 'Ha, ha' must be a really hearty laugh.

Hallowe'en

Upon that night, when fairies light
  On Cassilis Downans dance,   *hillocks of Cassilis, Kirkmichael*
Or owre the lays, in splendid blaze,
  On sprightly coursers prance;
Or for Colean the rout is taen,   *Culzean Castle, road*
  Beneath the moon's pale beams;
There, up the Cove, to stray and rove,   *Culzean Bay*
  Amang the rocks and streams
    To sport that night:

Amang the bonie winding banks,
  Where Doon rins, wimplin, clear: *winding*
Where Bruce ance ruled the martial ranks,   *Robert de Brus (1241-1304) father of King Robert I*
  An shook his Carrick spear;   *southern Ayrshire*
Some merry, friendly, country-folks
  Together did convene,
To burn their nits, an pou their stocks,   *nuts, pull, plants*
  An haud their Halloween   *keep*
    Fu blythe that night.

The lasses feat an cleanly neat,   *spruce*
  Mair braw than when they're fine;   *fair*
Their faces blythe fu sweetly kythe,   *show*
  Hearts leal, an warm, an kin: *loyal*
The lads sae trig, wi wooer-babs   *smart, love-knots*
  Weel-knotted on their garten;   *garters*
Some unco blate, an some wi gabs   *shy, talk*
  Gar lasses' hearts gang startin   *make*
    Whyles fast at night.   *sometimes*

'Ae hairst afore the Sherra-moor,   *harvest, Battle of Sheriffmuir 1715*
  I mind't as weel's yestreen –   *remember*
I was a gilpey then, I'm sure   *young girl*
  I was na past fyfteen:
The simmer had been cauld an wat,
  An stuff was unco green;   *grain*
An ay a rantin kirn we gat,   *rollicking, harvest-home*
  An just on Halloween
    It fell that night.

This a selection from a long poem telling of Halloween superstitions of the olden days. There is fear, humour and character in plenty. Give scope for all these moods. Narrative.

To a Mouse

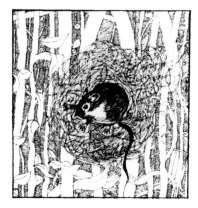

Wee sleekit, cow'rin, tim'rous beastie,   glossy-coated
O, what a panic's in thy breastie!
Thou need na start awa sae hasty,
      Wi bickering brattle!   rushing, scurry
I wad be laith to rin an chase thee,   loth
      Wi murdering pattle!   plough-scraper

I'm truly sorry man's dominion
Has broken Nature's social union,
An justifies that ill opinion,
      Which makes thee startle
At me, thy poor, earth-born companion,
      An fellow mortal!

I doubt na, whyles, but thou may thieve;   sometimes
What then? poor beastie, thou maun live!
A daimen icker in a thrave   odd ear in 24 sheaves
      'S a sma request;
I'll get a blessin wi the lave,   remainder
      An never miss't!

Thy wee-bit housie, too, in ruin!
Its silly wa's the win's are strewin!   feeble
An naething, now, to big a new ane,
      O foggage green!   coarse grass
An bleak December's win's ensuin,
      Baith snell an keen!   bitter

Thou saw the fields laid bare an waste,
An weary winter comin fast,
An cozie here, beneath the blast,
    Thou thought to dwell,
Till crash! the cruel coulter past   ploughshare
    Out thro thy cell.

That wee bit heap o leaves an stibble,   stubble
Has cost thee monie a' weary nibble!
Now thou's turn'd out, for a thy trouble,
    But house or hald,   without, holding
To thole the winter's sleety dribble,   endure
    An cranreuch cauld!   hoar-frost

But Mousie, thou art no thy lane,   alone
In proving foresight may be vain:
The best-laid schemes o mice an men
    Gang aft agley,   often go awry
An lea'e us nought but grief an pain,
    For promis'd joy!

Still thou art blest, compar'd wi me!
The present only toucheth thee:
But och! I backward cast my e'e,
    On prospects drear!
An forward, thou I canna see,
    I guess an fear!

One of Burns's best loved poems.
Try when speaking to see the mouse as Burns saw it.

The Deil's Awa Wi th' Exciseman

CHORUS
The Deil's awa, the Deil's awa,
  The Deil's awa wi th' Exciseman!
He's danc'd awa, he's danc'd awa,
  He's danc'd awa wi th' Exciseman!

The Deil cam fiddlin thro the town,
  And danc'd awa wi th' Exciseman,
And ilka wife cries:– 'Auld Mahoun,   every
  I wish you luck o the prize man!'

'We'll make our maut, and we'll brew our drink,   malt
  We'll laugh, sing, and rejoice, man,
And monie braw thanks to the meikle black Deil,   fine, great
  That danc'd awa wi th' Exciseman.

There's threesome reels, there's foursome reels,
  There's hornpipes and strathspeys, man,
But the ae best dance e'er cam to the land
  Was *The Deil's awa wi th' Exciseman.*

It is not necessary to point out the rhythms here – the feet tingle to the words. Lyric with a character.

What Can a Young Lassie Do Wi an Auld Man

What can a young lassie, what shall a young lassie,
  What can a young lassie do wi an auld man?
Bad luck on the penny that tempted my minnie   mother
  To sell her puir Jenny for siller an lan'!   money

He's always compleenin frae mornin to eenin;
  He hoasts and he hirples the weary day lang;   coughs, limps
He's doylt and he's dozin, his blude it is frozen –   senile
  O, dreary's the night wi a crazy auld man!

He hums and he hankers, he frets and he cankers,   crabs
  I never can please him do a' that I can.
He's peevish an jealous o a' the young fellows –
  O, dool on the day I met wi an auld man!   woe

My auld auntie Katie upon me taks pity,
  I'll do my endeavour to follow her plan;
I'll cross him an wrack him, until I heartbreak him,
  And then his auld brass will buy me a new pan.

There is opportunity to convey the couthy shy humour in this poem. Lyric with humour.

The Tarbolton Lasses

If ye gae up to yon hill-tap,
    Ye'll there see bonie Peggy:
She kens her father is a laird,
    And she forsooth's a leddy.   lady

There's Sophie tight, a lassie bright,   prepared or dressed
    Besides a handsome fortune:
Wha canna win her in a night,
    Has little art in courtin.

Gae down by Faile, and taste the ale,
    And tak a look o Mysie:
She's dour and din, a deil within,   stubborn, swarthy
    But aiblins she may please ye.   perhaps

If she be shy, her sister try,
    Ye'll may be fancy Jenny:
If ye'll dispense wi want o sense
    She kens herself she's bonie.

As ye gae up by yon hillside,   that
    Spier in for bonie Bessy: call
She'll gie ye a beck, and bid ye light,   curtsy
    And handsomely address ye.

There's few sae bonie, nane sae guid
    In a' King George' dominion:
If ye should doubt the truth o this,
    It's Bessy's ain opinion!

A fine final verse. It needs the right cadence to present Bessie's opinion. Lyric.

Green Grow the Rashes O,

CHORUS
Green grow the rashes, O;
  Green grow the rashes, O;
The sweetest hours that e'er I spend,
  Are spent among the lasses, O.

There's nought but care on ev'ry han',
  In every hour that passes, O:
What signifies the life o man,
  An 'twere na for the lasses, O.

The war'ly race may riches chase,   wordly
  An riches still may fly them, O;
An tho at last they catch them fast,
  Their hearts can ne'er enjoy them, O.

But gie me a cannie hour at e'en,   quiet, evening
  My arms about my dearie, O,
An war'ly cares an war'ly men,
  May a' gae tapsalteerie, O!   topsy-turvy

For you sae douce, ye sneer at this;   sober
  Ye're nought but senseless asses, O:
The wisest man the warl' e'er saw,
  He dearly lov'd the lasses, O.

Auld Nature swears, the lovely dears
  Her noblest work she classes, O:
Her prentice han' she try'd on man,
  An then she made the lasses, O.

This is a fine poem with opportunity to give a different tone to each verse. A lyric but must be given character.

Now Westlin Winds

Now westlin winds and slaught'ring guns   western
   Bring Autumn's pleasant weather;
The moorcock springs on whirring wings
   Amang the blooming heather:
Now waving grain, wide o'er the plain,
   Delights the weary farmer;
And the moon shines bright, as I rove by night
   To muse upon my charmer.

The paitrick lo'es the fruitfu fells,   partridge
   The plover lo'es the mountains;
The woodcock haunts the lonely dells,
   The soaring hern the fountains: heron
Thro lofty groves the cushat roves,   pigeon
   The path o man to shun it;
The hazel bush o'erhangs the thrush,
   The spreading thorn the linnet.

But, Peggy dear, the eve'ning's clear,
   Thick flies the skimming swallow;
The sky is blue, the fields in view,
   All fading-green and yellow:
Come let us stray our gladsome way,
   And view the charms of Nature;
The rustling corn, the fruited thorn,
   And ilka happy creature.   every

We'll gently walk, and sweetly talk,
   While the silent moon shines clearly;
I'll clasp thy waist, and fondly prest,
   Swear how I lo'e thee dearly:
Not vernal show'rs to budding flow'rs,
   Not Autumn to the farmer,
So dear can be as thou to me,
   My fair, my lovely charmer!

Here we have a poem which is a masterly description of Nature. Every phrase must be eloquent. Lyric.

John Anderson, My Jo

John Anderson my jo, John,   *darling*
  When we were first acquent,   *acquainted*
Your locks were like the raven,
  Your bonie brow was brent;   *smooth*
But now your brow is beld, John,   *bald*
  Your locks are like the snaw,
But blessing on your frosty pow,   *pate*
  John Anderson, my jo!

John Anderson my jo, John,
  We clamb the hill thegither,   *climbed, together*
And monie a cantie day, John,   *happy*
  We've had wi ane anither;
Now we maun totter down, John,   *must*
  And hand in hand we'll go,
And sleep thegither at the foot,
  John Anderson my jo!

The lovely thoughts in this poem call for sincerity of speech. Lyrics.

The Chevalier's Lament

The small birds rejoice in the green leaves returning,
The murmuring streamlet winds clear thro the vale,
The primroses blow in the dews of the morning,
And wild scatter'd cowslips bedeck the green dale:
But what can give pleasure, or what can seem fair,
When the lingering moments are number'd by care?
No flow'rs gaily springing, nor birds sweetly singing,
Can soothe the sad bosom of joyless despair!

The deed that I dar'd, could it merit their malice,
A king and a father to place on his throne?
His right are these hills, and his right are those valleys,
Where the wild beasts find shelter, tho I can find none!
But 'tis not my suff'rings this wretched, forlorn –
My brave gallant friends, 'tis your ruin I mourn!
Your faith prov'd so loyal in hot bloody trial,
Alas! can I make it no better return?

To obtain the right mood of this poem it is necessary
to know that 'Bonnie Prince Charlie' is speaking.
Lyrical lyric.

Tam O' Shanter

Care, mad to see a man sae happy,
E'en drown'd himsel amang the nappy.
As bees flee hame wi lades o treasure,   loads
The minutes wing'd their way wi pleasure:
Kings may be blest but Tam was glorious,
O'er a' the ills o life victorious!

But pleasures are like poppies spread:
You seize the flow'r, its bloom is shed;
Or like the snow falls in the river,
A moment white – then melts for ever;
Or like the borealis race,   Aurora or Northern Lights
That flit ere you can point their place;
Or like the rainbow's lovely form
Evanishing amid the storm.
Nae man can tether time or tide,
The hour approaches Tam maun ride: must
That hour, o night's black arch the key-stane,
That dreary hour Tam mounts his beast in:
And sic a night he taks the road in,   such
As ne'er poor sinner was abroad in.

The wind blew as 'twad blawn its last;   would have blown
The rattling showers rose on the blast;
The speedy gleams the darkness swallow'd;
Loud, deep, and lang the thunder bellow'd;
That night, a child might understand,
The Deil had business on his hand.

Note the change from Scots to English, a clever device of Burns. Narrative.

61

Tam Glen

My heart is a-breaking, dear tittie,   sister
   Some counsel unto me come len',
To anger them a' is a pity,
   But what will I do wi Tam Glen?

I'm thinking, wi sic a braw fellow,   fine
   In poortith I might make a fen';   poverty, shift
What care I in riches to wallow,
   If I mauna marry Tam Glen?   must not

There's Lowrie the laird o Dumeller:
   'Guid day to you' – brute! he comes ben,
He brags and he blaws o his siller,
   But when will he dance like Tam Glen?

My minnie does constantly deave me,   mother, deafen
   And bids me beware o young men.
They flatter, she says, to deceive me –
   But wha can think sae o Tam Glen?

My daddie says, gin I'll forsake him,   if
   He'd gie me guid hunder marks ten.   £55 sterling
But if it's ordain'd I maun take him,
   O, wha will I get but Tam Glen?

Yestreen at the Valentines' dealing,
   My heart to my mou gied a sten,   mouth, start
For thrice I drew ane without failing,
   And thrice it was written 'Tam Glen!'

The last Hallowe'en I was waukin
   My droukit sark-sleeve, as ye ken –   drenched, shirt-sleeve
His likeness came up the house staukin,   stalking
   And the very grey breeks o Tam Glen!   breeches

Come, counsel, dear tittie, don't tarry!
   I'll gie ye my bonie black hen,
Gif ye will advise me to marry
   The lad I lo'e dearly, Tam Glen.

A poem with persuasive tone. Endeavour to make it so. Lyric spoken by the young girl.

The Lass of Cessnock Banks

On Cessnock banks a lassie dwells,
   Could I describe her shape and mien!
Our lasses a' she far excels –
   An she has twa sparkling, rogueish een!   eyes

She's sweeter than the morning dawn,
   When rising Phoebus first is seen,
And dew-drops twinkle o'er the lawn –
   An she has twa sparkling, rogueish een!

She's stately like yon youthful ash,   yonder
   That grows the cowslip braes between,   hillsides
And drinks the stream with vigour fresh –
   An she has twa sparkling, rogueish een!

She's spotless like the flow'ring thorn,
   With flow'rs so white and leaves so green,
When purest in the dewy morn –
   An she has twa sparkling, rogueish een!

Her looks are like the vernal May,
   When ev'ning Phoebus shines serene,
While birds rejoice on every spray –
   An she has twa sparkling, rogueish een!

Her hair is like the curling mist,
   That climbs the mountain-sides at e'en,
When flow'r-reviving rains are past –
   An she has twa sparkling, rogueish een!

Her forehead's like the show'ry bow,
   When gleaming sunbeams intervene,
And gild the distant mountain's brow –
   An she has twa sparkling, rogueish een!

Her cheeks are like yon crimson gem,
   The pride of all the flowery scene,
Just opening on its thorny stem –
   An she has twa sparkling, rogueish een!

But it's not her air, her form, her face,
   Tho matching Beauty's fabled Queen:
'Tis the mind that shines in ev'ry grace –
   An chiefly in her rogueish een!

Care must be taken here to give the climax
of the poem in the last verse. Lyric.

The Twa Dogs

'Twas in that place o Scotland's Isle, Kyle
That bears the name of auld King Coil,
Upon a bonie day in June,
When wearin thro the afternoon,
Twa dogs, that were na thrang at hame, busy
Forgathered ance upon a time. encountered
 The first I'll name, they ca'd him Caesar,
Was keepit for 'his Honor's' pleasure:
His hair, his size, his mouth, his lugs, ears
Shew'd he was nane o Scotland's dogs;
But whalpit someplace far abroad, pupped
Whare sailors gang to fish for cod. Newfoundland
 His locked, letter'd, braw brass collar
Shew'd him the gentleman an scholar;
But tho he was o high degree, devil
The fient a pride, nae pride had he; other

The tither was a ploughman's collie,
A rhyming, ranting, raving billie, fellow
Wha for his friend an comrade had him,
And in his freaks had Luath ca'd him,
After some dog in Highland sang, MacPherson's Ossian – a sly dig at this literary forgery
Was made lang syne – Lord knows how lang.
 He was a gash an faithfu tyke, respectable
An ever lap a sheugh or dyke. ditch, stone wall
His honest, sonsie, baws'nt face pleasant, white-streaked
Ay gat him friends in ilka place; Always, every
His breast is white, his tousie back shaggy
Weel clad wi coat o glossy black;
His gawsie tail; wi upward curl, jolly
Hung owre his hurdies wi a swirl. buttocks

A fine poem in which to use a strong narrative characteristic quality.

Scots Wha Hae

Scots, wha hae wi Wallace bled,
Scots, wham Bruce has aften led,
Welcome to your gory bed
      Or to victorie!
Now's the day, and now's the hour:
See the front o battle lour,
See approach proud Edward's power –
      Chains and slaverie!

Wha will be a traitor knave?
Wha can fill a coward's grave?
Wha sae base as be a slave? –
      Let him turn, and flee!
Wha for Scotland's King and Law
Freedom's sword will strongly draw
Freeman stand, or Freeman fa',
      Let him follow me!

By Oppression's woes and pains,
By your sons in servile chains,
We will drain your dearest veins,
      But they shall be free!
Lay the proud usurpers low!
Tyrants fall in every foe!
Liberty's in every blow! –
      Let us do, or die!

Sir William Wallace (d.1305)
King Robert I (1306-28)

look menacingly
Edward II (1307-27)

A real Scottish anthem in this poem. It needs a real Scottish fervour. A lyrical narrative.

A Man's a Man for a' That

Is there for honest poverty
  That hings his head, an a' that?   hangs
The coward slave, we pass him by –
  We dare be poor for a' that!
For a' that, an a' that,
  Our toils obscure, an a' that,
The rank is but the guinea's stamp,
  The man's the gowd for a' that.   gold

What though on hamely fare we dine,
  Wear hoddin grey, an a' that?   coarse woolen cloth
Gie fools their silks, and knaves their wine –
  A man's a man for a' that.
For a' that, an a' that,
  Their tinsel show, an a' that,
The honest man, tho e'er sae poor,
  Is king o men for a' that.

Ye see yon birkie ca'd 'a lord,'   fellow
  Wha struts, an stares, an a' that?
Tho hundreds worship at his word,
  He's but a cuif for a' that.   fool
For a' that, an a' that,
  His ribband, star, an a' that,
The man o independent mind,
  He looks an laughs at a' that.

A prince can mak a belted knight,
  A marquis, duke, an a' that!   above
But an honest man's aboon his might –   must not
  Guid faith, he mauna fa' that!
For a' that, an a' that,
  Their dignities, an a' that,
The pith o sense an pride o worth,
  Are higher rank than a' that.

Then let us pray that come it may
  (As come it will for a' that),
That Sense and Worth o'er a' the earth,
  Shall bear the gree an a' that.   have priority
For a' that, an a' that,
  It's comin yet for a' that,
That man to man, the world, o'er
  Shall brithers be for a' that.

A fine robust poem demanding a robust delivery. Narrative.

McPherson's Farewell

CHORUS
Sae rantingly, sae wantonly,
Sae dauntingly gaed he,   went
He play'd a spring, and danc'd it round
Below the gallows-tree.

Farewell ye dungeons dark and strong,
    The wretch's destinie!
McPherson's time will not be long
    On yonder gallows-tree.

O what is death but parting breath?
    On many a bloody plain
I've dared his face, and in this place
    I scorn him yet again!

Untie these bands from off my hands,
    And bring to me my sword,
And there's no a man in all Scotland
    But I'll brave him at a word.

I've liv'd a life of sturt and strife;   trouble
    I die by treacherie:
It burns my heart I must depart,
    And not avenged be.

Now farewell light, thou sunshine bright,
    And all beneath the sky!
May coward shame distain his name,
    The wretch that dare not die!

McPherson was a brave man – give the poem a mood of gallantry. Narrative.

NEW BRIG

'Auld Vandal! ye but show your little mense,
Just much about it wi your scanty sense:
Will your poor, narrow foot-path of a street,
Where twa wheel-barrows tremble when they meet,
Your ruin'd, formless bulk o stane an lime,
Compare wi bonie brigs o modern time?
There's men o taste would tak the Ducat stream,
Tho they should cast the vera sark and swim,
E'er they would grate their feelings wi the view
O sic an ugly, Gothic hulk as you.'

AULD BRIG

'Conceited gowk! puffed up wi windy pride!	cuckoo
This monie a year I've stood the flood an tide;	
And tho wi crazy eild I'm sair forfairn,	eld, worn out
I'll be a brig when ye're a shapeless cairn!	
As yet ye little ken about the matter,	
But twa-three winters will inform ye better.	
When heavy, dark, continued, a'-day rains	day-long
Wi deepening deluges o'erflow the plains;	
When from the hills where springs the brawling Coil,	four tributaries of the River Ayr
Or stately Lugar's mossy fountains boil,	
Or where the Greenock winds his moorland course,	
Or haunted Garpal draws his feeble source,	
Arous'd by blustering winds an spotting thowes,	thaws
In monie a torrent down the snaw-broo rowes;	snow-brew rolls
While crashing ice, borne on the roaring speat,	flood
Sweeps dams, an mills, an brigs, a' to the gate;	
And from Glenbuck down to the Ratton-Key.	village in Muirkirk parish
Auld Ayr is just one lengthen'd tumbling sea –	
Then down ye'll hurl (deil nor ye never rise!),	crash
And dash the gumlie jaups up to the pouring skies!	muddy splashes
A lesson sadly teaching, to your cost,	
That Architecture's noble art is lost!'	

Here point out the old architecture is much sturdier than the new. Two different voices will help. Narrative.

The Death and Dying Words of Poor Mailie

As Mailie, an her lambs thegither,   together
Was ae day nibblin on the tether,
Upon her cloot she coost a hitch,   hoof, looped
An owre she warsl'd in the ditch: floundered
There, groanin, dying, she did lie,
When Hughoc he cam doytin by.   staggering

  Wi glowrin een, and lifted han's   staring
Poor Hughoc like a statue stan's;
He saw her days were near-hand ended,
But, wae's my heart! he could na mend it!   woe
He gaped wide, but naething spak,
At length poor Mailie silence brak:–

  'O thou, whase lamentable face
Appears to mourn my woefu case!
My dying words attentive hear,
An bear them to my Master dear.

  Tell him, if e'er again he keep   own
As muckle gear as buy a sheep –   much money
O, bid him never tie them mair,
Wi wicked strings o hemp or hair!
But ca' them out to park or hill,   drive
An let them wander at their will:
So may his flock increase, an grow
To scores o lambs, and packs o woo'!

'Tell him, he was a Master kin',
An ay was guid to me an mine;
An now my dying charge I gie him,
My helpless lambs, I trust them wi him.

'An niest, my yowie, silly thing,   next
Gude keep thee frae a tether string!
O, may thou ne'er forgather up,   make friends
Wi onie blastit, moorland toop;
But ay keep mind to moop an mell,   nibble and meddle
Wi sheep o credit like thysel!

'And now, my bairns, wi my last breath,
I lea'e my blessin wi you baith:
An when you think upo your mither,
Mind to be kind to ane anither.

'Now, honest Hughoc, dinna fail,
To tell my master a' my tale;
An bid him burn this cursed tether,
An for thy pains thou'se get my blether.'   bladder

This said, poor Mailie turn'd her head,
An clos'd her een amang the dead!

Burns did find this sheep dying. There is an opportunity to adopt a conversational delivery here. Narrative.

Lord Gregory

O, mirk, mirk is this midnight hour,
  And loud the tempest's roar!
A waefu wanderer seeks thy tower –
  Lord Gregory, ope thy door.
An exile frae her father's ha',
  And a' for sake o thee,
At least some pity on me shaw,
  If love it may na be.

Lord Gregory mind'st thou not the grove
  By bonie Irwine side,
Where first I own'd that virgin love
  I lang, lang had denied?
How aften didst thou pledge and vow,
  Thou wad for ay be mine!
And found my heart, itsel sae true,
  It ne'er mistrusted thine.

Hard is thy heart, Lord Gregory,
  And flinty is thy breast:
Thou bolt of Heaven that flashest by,
  O, wilt thou bring me rest!
Ye mustering thunders from above,
  Your willing victim see,
But spare and pardon my fause love,
  His wrangs to Heaven and me!

Mark the change in each verse by a new attack.

O, Wert Thou in the Caul Blast

This poem was written just before he died for
Jessie Lewars who nursed him to the end.

O, wert thou in the cauld blast
  On yonder lea, on yonder lea,
My plaidie to the angry airt,
  I'd shelter thee, I'd shelter thee.
Or did Misfortune's bitter storms
  Around thee blaw, around thee blaw,
Thy bield should be my bosom,
  To share it a', to share it a'.

Or were I in the wildest waste,
  Sae black and bare, sae black and bare,
The desert were a Paradise,
  If thou wert there, if thou wert there.
Or were I monarch o the globe,
  Wi thee to reign, wi thee to reign,
The brightest jewel in my crown
  Wad be my queen, wad be my queen.

The Country Lass

In simmer, when the hay was mawn   *mown*
  And corn wav'd green in ilka field,   *every*
While claver blooms white o'er the ley   *clover meadow*
  And roses blaw in ilka bield   *shelter*
Blythe Bessie in the milking shiel   *shieling*
  Says:– 'I'll be wed, come o't what will!'
Out spake a dame in wrinkled eild:–   *eld*
  'O guid advisement comes nae ill.

'It's ye hae wooers monie ane,   *many a one*
  And lassie, ye're but young, ye ken!   *know*
Then wait a wee, and cannie wale   *bit, prudently choose*
  A routhie butt, a routhie ben.   *well-stocked kitchen, parlour*
There's Johnie o the Buskie-Glen,
  Fu is his barn, fu is his byre.   *cow-shed*
Take this frae me, my bonie hen:
  It's plenty beets the luver's fire!'   *fans*

'For Johnie o the Buskie-Glen
  I dinna care a single flie:
He lo'es sae weel his craps and kye,   *crops, cows*
  He has nae love to spare for me,
But blythe's the blink o Robie's e'e,
  And weel I wat he lo'es me dear:
Ae blink o him I wad na gie   *one glimpse*
  For Buskie-Glen and a' his gear.'

'O thoughtless lassie, life's a faught!   *fight*
  The canniest gate, the strife is sair.   *quietest way, sore*
But ay fu-han't is fechtin best: *full-handed, fighting*
  A hungry care's an unco care.
But some will spend and some will spare,
  An wilfu folk maun hae their will.   *must*
Syne as ye brew, my maiden fair,
  Keep mind that ye maun drink the yill!'   *ale*

'O gear will buy me rigs o land,
  And gear will buy me sheep and kye!
But the tender heart o leesome loove   *lawful*
  The gowd and siller canna buy!   *gold, silver*
We may be poor, Robie and I;
  Light is the burden luve lays on;
Content and loove brings peace and joy:
  What mair hae Queens upon a throne?'

An excellent chance to create a character here who knows her man. Narrative. An old wife and a lassie.

73

The Bonnie Lass of Albanie

My heart is wae, and unco wae,   *mighty sad*
   To think upon the raging sea,
That roars between her gardens green
   An the bonie lass of Albanie.

This lovely maid's of royal blood,
   That ruled Albion's kingdoms three;   *England, Scotland and Ireland*
But Oh, alas for her bonie face!
   They hae wrang'd the lass of Albanie.

In the rolling tide of spreading Clyde
   There sits an isle of high degree,   *the isle of Bute*
And a town of fame, whose princely name   *Rothesay*
   Should grace the lass of Albanie.

But there is a youth, a witless youth,   *Prince George,*
   That fills the place where she should be;   *later Prince Regent and King George IV*
We'll send him o'er to his native shore,
   And bring our ain sweet Albanie!

Alas the day, and woe the day!
   A false usurper wan the gree,   *highest honors*
Who now commands the towers and lands,
   The royal right of Albanie.

We'll daily pray, we'll nightly pray,
   On bended knees most fervently,
The time may come, with pipe and drum
   We'll welcome hame fair Albanie.

True to ballad forms each verse stands alone. A new attack at each verse is necessary.

To the Guidwife of Wauchope House

I mind it weel, in early date, — remember
When I was beardless, young, and blate, — bashful
  An first could thresh the barn,
Or haud a yokin at the pleugh, — hold, a day's work
An tho forfoughten sair eneugh, — exhausted
  Yet unco proud to learn; — mighty
When first amang the yellow corn
  A man I reckon'd was,
An wi the lave ilk merry morn — others, each
  Could rank my rig an lass: — ridge
    Still shearing, and clearing — reaping
      The tither stooked raw, — row of sheaves
    Wi clavers an havers, — gossip, nonsense
      Wearing the day awa. — away

E'en then, a wish (I mind its pow'r),
A wish that to my latest hour
  Shall strongly heave my breast,
That I for poor auld Scotland's sake
Some usefu plan or book could make,
  Or sing a sang at least.
The rough burr-thistle spreading wide
  Amang the bearded bear, — barley
I turn'd the weeder-clips aside, — shears
  An spar'd the symbol dear.
    No nation, no station,
      My envy e'er could raise;
    A scot still, but blot still, — without
      I knew nae higher praise.

For you, no bred to barn and byre, — cow-shed
Wha sweetly tune the Scottish lyre,
  Thanks to you for your line!
The marl'd plaid ye kindly spare, — parti-coloured
By me should gratefully be ware; — worn
  'Twad please me to the nine. — perfection
I'd be mair vauntie o my hap, — proud, covering
  Douce hingin owre my curple, — soberly, crupper
Than onie ermine ever lap, — folded
Or proud imperial purple.
    Farewell then! Lang hale then, — long heath
      An plenty be your fa! — lot
    May losses and crosses
      Ne'er at your hallan ca'! — porch

This is one of Burns's many epistles. It must be thoughtful, never dramatised. A lyrical epistle with a personal note.

75

The Soldier's Return

When wild War's deadly blast was blawn,
  And gentle Peace returning,
Wi monie a sweet babe fatherless
  And monie a widow mourning,
I left the lines and tented field,
  Where lang I'd been a lodger,
My humble knapsack a' may wealth,
  A poor but honest sodger.   soldier

A leal, light heart was in my breast,   true
  My hand unstain'd wi plunder,
And for fair Scotia, hame again,
  I cheery on did wander:
I thought upon the banks o Coil,
  I thought upon my Nancy,
And ay I mind't the witching smile
  That caught my youthful fancy.

At length I reach'd the bonie glen,
  Where early life I sported.
I pass'd the mill and trysting thorn,
  Where Nancy aft I courted.
Wha spied I but my ain dear maid,
  Down by her mother's dwelling,
And turn'd me round to hide the flood
  That in my e'en was swelling!

Wi alter'd voice, quoth I:– 'Sweet lass,
  Sweet as yon hawthorn's blossom,
O, happy, happy may he be,
  That's dearest to thy bosom!
My purse is light, I've far to gang,
  And fain would be thy lodger:
I've served my king and country lang –
  Take pity on a sodger'.

Sae wistfully she gaz'd on me,
    And lovelier was than ever.
Quo she – 'A sodger ance I lo'ed,
    Forget him shall I never:
Our humble cot, and hamely fare,
    Ye freely shall partake it;
That gallant badge – the dear cockade –
    Ye're welcome for the sake o't!'

She gaz'd, she redden'd like a rose,
    Syne, pale like onie lily,   *Then*
She sank within my arms, and cried:–
    'Art thou my ain dear Willie?'
'By Him who made yon sun and sky,
    By whom true love's regarded,
I am the man! And thus may still
    True lovers be rewarded!

'The wars are o'er, and I'm come hame,
    And find thee still true-hearted.
Tho poor in gear, we're rich in love,   *wealth*
    And mair, we'se ne'er be parted.'
Quo she:– 'My grandsire left me gowd,   *gold*
    A mailen plenish'd fairly!   *farm, well-stocked*
And come, my faithfu sodger lad,
    Thou'rt welcome to it dearly!'

For gold the merchant ploughs the main,
    The farmer ploughs the manor;
But glory is the sodger's prize,
    The sodger's wealth is honour!
The brave poor sodger ne'er despise,
    Nor count him as a stranger:
Remember he's his country's stay
    In day and hour of danger.

A romantic story. It must have a new attack on each verse, moving quickly from place, scene and situation.

Epistle to J. Lapraik

An old Scottish Bard – April 1, 1785

I am nae poet, in a sense;
But just a rhymer like by chance.
An hae to learning nae pretence;
    Yet, what the matter?
Whene'er my Muse does on me glance,
    I jingle at her.

Your critic-folk may cock their nose,
And say, 'How can you e'er propose,
You wha ken hardly verse frae prose,
    To mak a sang?'
But, by your leaves, my learned foes,
    Ye're maybe wrang.

What's a' your jargon o your schools,
Your Latin names for horns an stools?
If honest Nature made you fools,
    What sairs your grammars?   serves
Ye'd better taen up spades and shools,   shovels
    Or knappin-hammers.   stone-breaking

A set o dull, conceited hashes   fools
Confuse their brains in college-classes,
They gang in stirks, and come out asses,   bullocks
    Plain truth to speak;
An syne they think to climb Parnassus   then
    By dint o Greek!

Gie me ae spark o Nature's fire,
That's a' the learning I desire;
Then, tho I drudge thro dub an mire   puddle
    At pleugh or cart,
My Muse, tho hamely in attire,
    May touch the heart.

A fine Epistle in a fine rhythm – to be spoken as the poet would write. Lyrical Epistle (letter).

Thou whom chance may hither lead,
Be thou clad in russet weed,
Be thou deckt in silken stole,
Grave these counsels on thy soul.

Life is but a day at most,
Sprung from night, – in darkness lost;
Hope not sunshine ev'ry hour,
Fear not clouds will always lour.

As Youth and Love, with sprightly dance
Beneath thy morning star advance,
Pleasure with her siren air
Mey delude the thoughtless pair:
Let Prudence bless Enjoyment's cup,
Then raptur'd sip, and sip it up.

The smile or frown of awful Heav'n,
To Virtue or to Vice is giv'n;
Say, to be just, and kind, and wise –
There solid self-enjoyment lies;
That foolish, selfish, faithless ways
Lead to be wretched, vile, and base.

Thus resign'd and quiet, creep
To the bed of lasting sleep:
Sleep, whence thou shalt ne'er awake,
Night, where dawn shall never break;
Till future life, future no more,
To light and joy the good restore,
To light and joy unkown before.
Stranger, go! Heav'n be thy guide!
Quod the Beadsman of Nithside.

A reverie written while musing in the little sandstone summerhouse at Friars' Carse. Give it a thoughtful mood. Lyric.

Tam Lin

O I forbid you, maidens a'   gold
   That wear gowd on your hair,   go
To come, or gae by Carterhaugh,
   For young Tom-lin is there.

Janet has kilted her green kirtle,   petticoat
   A little aboon her knee;   above
And she has broded her yellow hair   braided
   A little aboon her bree;   brow
And she's awa to Carterhaugh
   As fast as she can hie.

When she cam to Carterhaugh
   Tom-lin was at the well,
And there she fand his steed standing   found
   But away was himsel.

She had na pu'd a double rose,   plucked
   A rose but only tway,   two
Till up then started young Tom-lin,
   Says, Lady, thou's pu nae mae.

Why pu's thou the rose, Janet,
   And why breaks thou the wand?
Or why comes thou to Carterhaugh
   Withoutten my command?

Carterhaugh it is my ain,   own
   Ma daddie gave it me;
I'll come and gang by Carterhaugh
   And ask nae leave at thee.

O tell me, Tom-lin she says,
   For's sake that died on tree,
If e'er ye was in holy chapel,
   Or Christendom did see.

Ance it fell upon a day,
   A cauld day and a snell,
When we were frae the hunting come   bitter
   That frae my horse I fell.

The queen o Fairies she caught me,
   In yon green hill to dwell,   that
And pleasant is the fairy-land;
   But, an eerie tale to tell!   strange

But the night is Halloween, lady,
    The morn is Hallowday;
Then win me, win me, an ye will,
    For weel I wat ye may.

Just at the mirk and midnight hour   dark
    The fairy folk will ride;
And they that wad their truelove win,   would
    At Milescross they maun bide.

But how shall I thee ken, Tom-lin,
    O how my truelove know,
Amang sae mony unco knights   mighty
    The like I never saw.

O first let pass the black, Lady,
    And syne let pass the brown;   then
But quickly run to the milk-white steed,
    Pu ye his rider down:

For I'll ride on the milk-white steed,
    And ay nearest the town;
Because I was an earthly knight
    They gie me that renown.

My right hand will be glov'd, lady,
    My left hand will be bare;
Cockt up shall my bonnet be,
    And kaim'd down shall my hair;   combed
And thae's the tokens I gie thee   those are
    Nae doubt I will be there.

Again they'll turn me in your arms
    To a red het gaud of airn;   hot goad iron
But hold me fast and fear me not,
    I'll do you nae harm.

And last they'll turn me, in your arms,
    Into the burning lead;
Then throw me into well-water,
    O throw me in wi speed!

Out then spak the queen o Fairies,
  And an angry queen was she;
Shame betide her ill-fard face,
  And an ill death may she die,
For she's ta'en awa the boniest knight
  In a' my companie.

This is an ancient Border Ballad reworked by Burns.

Lament of Mary Queen of Scots

on the Approach of Spring

Now Nature hangs her mantle green
  On every blooming tree,
And spreads her sheets o daises white
  Out o'er the grassy lea;
Now Phoebus cheers the crystal streams,
  And glads the azure skies:
But nought can glad the weary wight
  That fast in durance lies.

Now laverocks wake the merry morn,   larks
  Aloft on dewy wing;
The merle, in his noontide bow'r,   hawk
  Makes woodland echoes ring;

The mavis wild wi monie note,
  Sings drowsy day to rest:
In love and freedom they rejoice,
  Wi care nor thrall opprest.

Now blooms the lily by the bank,
  The primrose down the brae,
The hawthorn's budding in the glen,
  And milk-white is the slae:
The meanest hind in fair Scotland
  May rove their sweets amang;
But I, the Queen of a' Scotland,
  Maun lie in prison strang.   must

I was the Queen o bonie France,
  Where happy I hae been;
Fu lightly rase I in the morn,   rose
  As blythe lay down at e'en:
And I'm the sovereign of Scotland,
  And monie a traitor there;
Yet here I lie in foreign bands,
  And never-ending care.

But as for thee, thou false woman,
  My sister and my fae,
Grim vengeance yet shall whet a sword
  That thro thy soul shall gae!
The weeping blood in woman's breast
  Was never known to thee;
Nor th' balm that drops on wounds of woe
  Frae woman's pitying e'e.

My son! My son! may kinder stars   King James VI and I
   Upon thy fortune shine;
And may those pleasures gild thy reign,
   That ne'er wad blink on mine!   would
God keep thee frae thy mother's faes,
   Or turn their hearts to thee;
And where thou meet'st thy mother's friend,
   Remember him for me!

O! soon, to me, may summer suns
   Nae mair light up the morn!
Nae mair to me the autumn winds
   Wave o'er the yellow corn!
And, in the narrow house of death,
   Let winter round me rave;
And the next flow'rs that deck the spring,
   Bloom on my peaceful grave.

A beautiful poem needing a sincere note of sadness. Lyric but narrative.

Epistle to Dr. Blacklock

Ellisland, 21st October 1789

Wow, but your letter made me vauntie!   *proud*
And are ye hale, and weel, and cantie?   *cheerful*
I kend it still, your wee bit jauntie   *knew, little excursion*
  Wad bring ye to: *set you up*
Lord send you ay as weel's I want ye,
  And then ye'll do!

But what do you think, my trusty fier?   *friend*
I'm turn'd a gauger – Peace be here!
Parnassian queires, I fear, I fear,   *choirs*
  Ye'll now disdain me,
And then my fifty pound a year
  Will little gain me!

I hae a wife and twa wee laddies;
They maun hae brose and brats o duddies: *must have, scraps of clothing*
Ye ken yoursels my heart right proud is –
  I need na vaunt –
But I'll sned besoms, thraw saugh woodies, *prune, brooms, weave, willow twigs*
  Before they want.

Lord help me thro this warld o care!
I'm weary-sick o't late and air!   *early*
Not but I hae a richer share
  Than monie ithers;
But why should ae man better fare,
  And a' men brithers?

But to conclude my silly rhyme
(I'm scant o verse and scant o time):
To make a happy fireside clime
  To weans and wife,   *children*
That's the true pathos and sublime
  Of human life.

Another narrative in style – dramatic speech should be avoided. Narrative.

Epistle to Davie, a Brother Poet

January

While winds frae aff Ben-Lomond blaw,
And bar the doors wi drivin snaw,
 And hing us owre the ingle,   hang over fire
I set me down to pass the time,
And spin verse or twa o rhyme,
 In hamely, westlin jingle: western
While frosty winds blaw in the drift,
 Ben to the chimla lug,   Right to the chimney corner
I grudge a wee the great-folk's gift,   a little
 That live sae bien an snug: prosperous
  I tent less, and want less   value
   Their roomy fire-side;
  But hanker, and canker,
   To see their cursed pride.

It's hardly in a body's pow'r,
To keep, at times, frae being sour,
 To see how things are shar'd;
How best o chiels are whyles in want,   chaps, sometimes
While coofs on countless thousands rant,   fools, roister
 And ken na how to ware't;   spend
But, Davie, lad, ne'er fash your head   trouble
 Tho we hae little gear;   wealth
We're fit to win our daily bread,
 As lang's we're hale and fier: sound
  'Mair spier na, nor fear na,'
   Auld age ne'er mind a feg;   fig
  The last o't, the warst o't,
   Is only but to beg.

It's no in titles nor in rank:
It's no in wealth like Lon'on Bank,
 To purchase peace and rest,
It's no in makin muckle, mair;   much, more
It's no in books, it's no in lear,   learning
 To make us truly blest:
If happiness hae not her seat
 An centre in the breast,
We may be wise, or rich, or great,
 But never can be blest!
  Nae treasures nor pleasures
   Could make us happy lang;
  The heart ay's the part ay
   That makes us right or wrang.

Another fine letter in verse with many
excellent observations. These need careful
emphasis. Narrative with a lyric quality.

My Father was a Farmer

My father was a farmer upon the Carrick border, O,
And carefully he bred me in decency and order, O.
He bade me act a manly part, though I had ne'er a farthing, O,
For without an honest manly heart, no man was worth regarding, O.

Then out into the world my course I did determine, O,
Tho to be rich was not my wish, yet to be great was charming, O.
My talents they were not the worst, nor yet my education, O,
Resolv'd was I, at least to try to mend my situation, O.

In many a way, and vain essay, I courted Fortune's favour, O:
Some cause unseen still stept between, to frustrate each endeavour, O.
Sometimes by foes I was o'erpower'd, sometimes by friends forsaken, O,
And when my hope was at the top, I still was worst mistaken, O.

Then sore harras'd, and tir'd at last, with Fortune's vain delusion, O,
I dropt my schemes, like idle dreams, and came to this conclusion, O –
The past was bad, and the future hid, its good or ill untried, O,
But the present hour was in my pow'r, and so I would enjoy it, O.

No help, nor hope, nor view had I, nor person to befriend me, O,
So I must toil, and sweat, and moil, and labour to sustain me, O.
To plough and sow, to reap and mow, my father bred me early, O:
For one, he said, to labour bred, was a match for Fortune fairly, O.

Thus all obscure, unknown, and poor, thro life I'm doom'd to wander, O,
Till down my weary bones I lay in everlasting slumber, O.
No view nor care, but shun whate'er might breed me pain or sorrow, O,
I live to-day as well's I may, regardless of to-morrow, O.

But cheerful still, I am as well as a monarch in his palace, O,
Tho Fortune's frown still hunts me down, with all her wonted malice, O:
I make indeed my daily bread, but ne'er can make it farther, O,
But, as daily bread is all I need, I do not much regard her, O.

When sometimes by my labour, I earn a little money, O,
Some unforeseen misfortune comes gen'rally upon me, O;
Mischance, mistake, or by neglect, or my good-natur'd folly, O:
But, come what will, I've sworn it still, I'll ne'er be melencholy, O.

All you who follow wealth and power with unremitting ardour, O,
The more in this you look for bliss, you leave your view the farther, O,
Had you the wealth Potosi boasts, or nations to adore you, O,   Latin American silvermine
A cheerful honest-hearted clown I will prefer before you, O.

The many phrases must be given full and varied inflection. Lyrical narrative.

Bonie Jean

There was a lass, and she was fair!
  At kirk and market to be seen
When a' our fairest maids were met,
  The fairest maid was bonie Jean.

And ay she wrought her country wark,
  And ay she sang sae merrilie:
The blythest bird upon the bush
  Had ne'er a lighter heart than she!

But hawks will rob the tender joys,
  That bless the little lintwhite's nest,   linnet
And frost will blight the fairest flowers,
  And love will break the soundest rest.

Young Robie was the brawest lad,   finest
  The flower and pride of a' the glen,
And he had owsen, sheep, and kye,   oxen, cattle
  And wanton naigies nine or ten.   horses

He gaed wi Jeanie to the tryste,   cattle-fair
  He danc'd wi Jeanie on the down,
And, lang ere witless Jeanie wist,   realised
  Her heart was tint, her peace was stown!   lost, stolen

As in the bosom of the stream,
  The moonbeam dwells at dewy e'en.
So, trembling pure, was tender love
  Within the breast of bonie Jean.

And now she works her country's wark,
  And ay she sighs wi care and pain,
Yet wist na what her ail might be,   ailment
  Or what wad make her weel again.   would

But did na Jeanie's heart loup light,   leap
  And didna joy blink in her e'e;   glance
As Robie tauld a tale of love
  Ae e'enin on the lily lea?

While monie a bird sang sweet o love,
  And monie a flower blooms o'er the dale,
His cheek to hers he aft did lay,
  And whisper'd thus his tender tale.

A happy ballad but the ballad
form must be retained. Lyric.

Willie Wastle

Willie Wastle dwalt on Tweed,
 The spot they ca'd it Linkumdoddie.
Willie was a wabster guid   weaver
 Could stown a clue wi onie body.   have stolen
He had a wife was dour and din,   stubborn, saturnine
 O, Tinkler Maidgie was her mither!
Sic a wife as Willie had,
 I wad na gie a button for her.

She has an e'e (she has but ane),   eye
 The cat has twa the very colour,
Five rusty teeth, forbye a stump,   as well as
 A clapper-tongue wad deave a miller;   deafen
A whiskin beard about her mou,   mouth
 Her nose and chin they threaten ither: each other
Sic a wife as Willie had,
 I wad na gie a button for her.

She's bow-hough'd, she's hem-shin'd, bandy-legged, shins like hams
 Ae limpin leg a hand-breed shorter; hand's-breadth
She's twisted right, she's twisted left,
 To balance fair in ilka quarter;   each
She has a hump upon her breast,
 The twin o that upon her shouther: shoulder
Sic a wife as Willie had,
 I wad na gie a button for her.

Auld baudrans by the ingle sits,   Old cat
 An wi her loof her face a-washin: paw
But Willie's wife is nae sae trig.   trim
 She dights her grunzie wi a hushion; wipes, snout, footless stocking
Her walie nieves like midden-creels,   ample fists
 Her face wad fyle the Logan Water: foul
Sic a wife as Willie had,
 I wad na gie a button for her.

Unlimited scope for character and humour in this poem. Narrative.

Bessy & Her Spinning Wheel

O, leeze me on my spinnin-wheel! — Blessings
And leeze me on my rock and reel, — distaff
Frae tap to tae that cleeds me bien, — clothes, snugly
And haps me fiel and warm at e'en! — covers, well
I'll set me down, and sing and spin, — sit
While laigh descends the summer sun, — low
Blest wi content, and milk and meal –
O, leeze me on my spinnin-wheel.

On ilka hand the burnies trot, — either, brooks
And meet below my theekit cot. — thatched cottage
The scented birk and hawthorn white — birch
Across the pool their arms unite,
Alike to screen the birdie's nest
And little fishes' caller rest. — cool
The sun blinks kindly in the biel, — glances, shelter
Where blythe I turn my spinnin-wheel.

On lofty aiks the cushats wail, — oaks, pigeons
And Echo cons the doolfu tale. — woeful
The lintwhites in the hazel braes, — linnets, slopes
Delighted, rival ither's lays.
The craik amang the claver hay, — corncrake, clover
The paitrick whirrin o'er the ley. — partridge, meadow
The swallow jinkin round my shiel, — darting, shieling
Amuse me at my spinnin-wheel.

Wi sma' to sell and less to buy,
Aboon distress, below envy, — Above
O, wha wad leave this humble state
For a' the pride of a' the great?
Amid their flaring, idle toys,
Amid their cumbrous, dinsome joys,
Can they the peace and pleasure feel
Of Bessy at her spinnin-wheel?

A really lovely poem full of sweet pastoral sentiment.
This must be projected.

Weel mounted on his grey mare Meg
A better never lifted leg,
Tam skelpit on thro dub and mire,   spanked, puddle
Despising wind, and rain, and fire;
Whes holding fast his guid blue bonnet,   Now
Whiles crooning o'er an auld Scots sonnet,
Whiles glow'ring round wi prudent cares,   staring
Lest bogles catch him unawares: bogies
Kirk-Alloway was drawing nigh,
Whare ghaists and houlets nightly cry.   ghosts, owls

When, glimmering thro the groaning trees,
Kirk-Alloway seem'd in a bleeze,
Tho ilka bore the beams were glancing.   every chink
And loud resounded mirth and dancing.

Warlocks and witches in a dance:
Nae cotillion, brent new frae France,   brand
But hornpipes, jigs, strathspeys, and reels,
Put life and mettle in their heels.

Till first ae caper, syne anither,   jerked then
Tam tint his reason a' thegither   lost
And roars out, 'Weel done, Cutty-sark!'
And in an instant all was dark:
And scarcely had he Maggie rallied,
When out the hellish legion sallied.

As eager runs the market-crowd,
When 'Catch the thief!' resounds aloud:
So Maggie runs, the witches follow,
Wi monie an eldritch skriech and hollow.   unearthly

Now, do thy speedy utmost, Meg,   bridge
And win the key-stane of the brig;
There, at them thou thy tail may toss,
A running stream they dare na cross!   not
But ere the key-stane she could make,
The fient a tail she had to shake,
For Nannie, far before the rest,
Hard upon noble Maggie prest,
And flew at Tam wi furious ettle;   aim
But little wist she Maggie's mettle!
Ae spring brought off her master hale,   whole
But left behind her ain grey tail:
The carlin claught her by the rump,   clawed
And left poor Maggie scarce a stump.

The verses arranged here give some feel of the poem which is well worth reading in its entirety.

The Auld Farmer's New Year Morning Salutation to His Auld Mare, Maggie

ON GIVING HER THE ACCUSTOMED RIPP OF CORN TO HANSEL IN THE NEW-YEAR

A Guid New-Year I wish thee, Maggie!
Hae, there's a ripp to thy auld baggie: *handful from sheaf, belly*
Tho thou's howebackit now, an knaggie, *hollow-backed, knobbly*
    I've seen the day
Thou could hae gaen like onie staggie, *gone, colt*
      Out-owre the lay. *lea*

Tho now thou's dowie, stiff an crazy, *drooping*
An thy auld hide as white's a daisie,
I've seen thee dappl't, sleek an glaizie, *glossy*
    A bonie gray:
He should been tight that daur't to raize thee, *ready, excite*
    Ance in a day.

Thou ance was i' the foremost rank,
A filly buirdly, steeve an swank: *elegant, trim, limber*
An set weel down a shapely shank,
    As e'er tread yird; *earth*
An could hae flown out-owre a stank, *pool*
    Like onie bird.

In cart or car thou never reestit;
The steyest brae thou wad hae fac't it; *steepest slope*
Thou never lap, an sten't, an breastit, *leaped, sprang*
    Then stood to blaw;
But just thy step a wee thing hastit,
    Thou snoov't awa. *jogged along*

My pleugh is now thy bairntime a', *ploughing-team, issue*
Four gallant brutes as e'er did draw;
Forbye sax mae I've sell't awa, *more*
    That thou hast nurst:
They drew my thretteen pund an twa,
    The vera warst.

The Auld Farmer's New Year Morning Salutation to His Auld Mare, Maggie (Contd.)

Monie a sair darg we twa hae wrought,   *hard day's work*
An wi the weary warl' fought!
An monie an anxious day, I thought
    We wad be beat!
Yet here to crazy age we're brought,
    Wi something yet.

An think na, my auld trusty servan',
That now perhaps thou's less deservin,
An my auld days may end in starvin;
    For my last fow,   *bushel*
A heapet stimpart, I'll reserve ane   *quarter of a peck*
    Laid by for you.

We've worn to crazy years thegither;
We'll toyte about wi ane anither;   *totter*
Wi tentie care I'll fit thy tether   *prudent, change*
    To some hain'd rig,   *reserved space*
Whare ye may nobly rax your leather,   *stretch your stomach*
    Wi sma' fatigue.

The salutation here and the king thoughts need careful reflections. Lyrical. The farmer speaks, but narrative in content.

Epistle to James Smith

Just now I've taen the fit o rhyme,
My barmie noddle's working prime,   seething brain
My fancy yerkit up sublime,   stirred
    Wi hasty summon:
Hae ye a leisure-moment's time
    To hear what's comin?

Some rhyme a neebor's name to lash;
Some rhyme (vain thought!) for needfu cash;
Some rhyme to court the countra clash,   talk
    An raise a din;
For me, an aim I never fash;   heed
    I rhyme for fun.

This life, sae far's I understand,
Is a' enchanted fairy-land.
Where Pleasure is the magic-wand,
    That, wielded right,
Maks hours like minutes, hand in hand,
    Dance by fu light.

O life! how pleasant, in thy morning,
Young Fancy's rays the hills adorning!
Cold-pausing Caution's lesson scorning,
    We frisk away,
Like school-boys, at th' expected warning,
    To joy an play.

We wander there, we wander here,
We eye the rose upon the brier,
Unmindful that the thorn is near,
    Among the leaves;
And tho the puny wound appear,
    Short while it grieves.

My pen I here fling to the door,
And kneel, ye Pow'rs! and warm implore,
'Tho I should wander *Terra* o'er,
    In all her climes,
Grant me but this, I ask no more,
    Ay rowth o rhymes.   plenty

Some humour here, needs that careful treatment for an epistle. Epistle.

O Tibbie, I Hae Seen the Day

O Tibbie, I hae seen the day,
  Ye wadna been sae shy! would not have been
For laik o gear ye lightly me, lack of wealth
  But, trowth, I care na by. I care not in return

Yestreen I met you on the moor, Last night
Ye spak na, but gaed by like stoure! went by like dust
Ye geck at me because I'm poor – toss your head
  But fient a hair care I! not

When comin hame on Sunday last,
Upon the road as I cam past,
Ye snifft an gae your head a cast – sniffed
  But, trowth, I care't na by! cared

I doubt na, lass, but ye may think,
Because ye hae the name o clink, money
That ye can please me at a wink,
  When'er ye like to try.

But sorrow tak him that's sae mean,
Altho his pouch o coin were clean,
Wha follows onie saucy quean, girl
  That looks sae proud and high!

Altho a lad were e'er sae smart,
If that he want the yellow dirt, money
Ye'll cast your head anither airt, direction
  And answer him fu dry.

But if he hae the name o gear,
Ye'll fasten to him like a brier,
Tho hardly he for sense or lear, learning
  Be better than the kye. cows

But, Tibbie, lass, tak my advice:
Your daddie's gear maks you sae nice,
The Deil a ane wad spier your price, ask
  Were ye as poor as I.

There lives a lass beside yon park,
I'd rather hae her in her sark shift
Than you wi a' your thousand mark,
  That gars you look sae high. makes

The good advice here should be spoken with admonition.

97

The Humble Petititon of Bruar Water

My lord, I know, your noble ear
  Woe ne'er assails in vain;
Embolden'd thus, I beg you'll hear
  Your humble slave complain,
How saucy Phoebus' scorching beams,
  In flaming summer-pride,
Dry-withering, waste my foamy streams.
  And drink my crystal tide.

The lightly-jumping, glowrin trouts,   staring
  That thro my waters play,
If, in their random, wanton spouts,
  They near the margin stray;
If, hapless chance! they linger lang,
  I'm scorching up so shallow,
They're left the whitening stanes amang
  In gasping death to wallow.

Here, foaming down the skelvy rocks,   shelving
  In twisting strength I rin;
There high my boiling torrent smokes,
  Wild-roaring o'er a linn: fall
Enjoying large each spring and well,
  As Nature gave them me,
I am, altho I say't mysel,
  Worth gaun a mile to see.   going

Would then, my noble master please
   To grant my highest wishes,
He'll shade my banks wi tow'ring trees
   And bonie spreading bushes.
Delighted doubly then, my lord,
   You'll wander on my banks,
And listen monie a grateful bird
   Return you tuneful thanks.

This is the water speaking – convey the mood that it wants shade.
A lovely last line needs a clever cadence. Lyric.

The Holy Fair

Upon a simmer Sunday morn,
  When Nature's face is fair,
I walked forth to view the corn,
  An snuff the caller air.   cool
The rising sun, owre Galston Muirs
  Wi glorious light was glintin;   glinting
The hares were hirplin down the furs, hopping, furrows
  The lav'rocks they were chantin   larks
      Fu sweet that day.

As lightsomely I glowr'd abroad,   gazed
  To see a scene sae gay,
Three hizzies, early at the road,   girls
  Cam skelpin up the way.   spanking along
Twa had manteels o dolefu black,
  But ane wi lyart lining;   grey
The third, that gaed a wee a-back,   walked a bit behind
  Was in the fashion shining,
      Fu gay that day.

The twa appear'd like sisters twin,
  In feature, form, an claes;   clothing
Their visage wither'd, lang and thin,
  An sour as onie slaes: blackthorn (sloes)
The third cam up, hap-step-an-lowp, hop, step and jump
  As light as onie lambie,
An wi a curchie low did stoop,   curtsey
  As soon as e'er she saw me,
      Fu kind that day.

Wi bonnet aff, quoth I, 'Sweet lass,
  I think ye seem to ken me;
I'm sure I've seen that bonie face,
  But yet I canna name ye.'

The Holy Fair was a religious festival held in Mauchline on the second Sunday in august.
There is an ample scope for character study here. Narrative.

The Inventory

In Answer to a Mandate by the Surveyor of Taxes

Sir, as your mandate did request,
I send you here a faithfu list
O guids an gear, an a' my graith, *chattles*
To which I'm clear to gi'e my aith. *oath*

 Imprimis, then, for carriage cattle: *cart-horses*
I hae four brutes o gallant mettle,
As ever drew before a pettle: *plough-scraper*
My *Lan'-afore's* a guide auld 'has been' *front left-hand horse*
An wight an wilfu a' his days been: *strong*
My *Lan'ahin's* a weel gaun fillie, *rear left-hand horse*
That aft has borne me hame frae Killie, *Kilmarnock*
An your auld borough monie a time, *Ayr*
In days when riding was nae crime.
But ance, when in my wooing pride
I, like a blockhead, boost to ride,
The wilfu creature sae I pat to, – *must, needs*
Lord pardon a' my sins, an that too!
I play'd my fillie sic a shavie, *trick*
She's a bedevil'd wi the spavie. *spavin*
My *Fur-ahins's* a wordy beast *rear furrow (right hand) worthy*
As e'er in tug or tow was traced.
The fourth's a Highland Donald hastie,
A damn'd red-wud Kilburnie blastie! *stark mad, Kilbirnie pest*
Foreby, a cowte, o cowtes the wale, *Besides, colt, pick*
As ever ran afore a tail:
If he be spar'd to be a beast,
He'll draw me fifteen pund at least. *fetch £15*
Wheel-carriages I ha'e but few,
Three carts, an twa are feckly new *partly*
An auld wheelbarrow – mair for token,
Ae leg an baith the trams are broken; *shafts*
I made a poker o the spin'le,
An my auld mither brunt the trin'le. *wheel*

 For men, I've three mischievous boys,
Run-deils for fechtin an for noise: *Right devils, fighting*
A gaudsman ane, a thrasher t'other, *cattle-drover*
Wee Davoc hauds the nowte in fother. *David Hutcheson / cattle, fodder*
I rule them, as I ought, discreetly,
An aften labour them completely;
An ay on Sundays duly, nightly,
I on the *Questions* tairge them tightly; *catechism, discipline*
Till, faith! wee Davoc's grown sae gleg, *sharp*
Tho scarcely langer than your leg.

101

But pray, remember, Mr. Aiken,   Robert Aiken
Nae kind o licence out I'm takin:
Sae dinna put me in your beuk,   do not, book
Nor for my ten white shillings leuk.

  This list wi my ain hand I've wrote it,
The day and date as under notit;
Then know all ye whom it concerns,

          Subscripsi huic,   ROBERT BURNS

It is not easy to enumerate a list of goods. It must be interesting by careful modulation. Narrative.

The Posie

O, luve will venture in where it daur na weel be seen!
O, luve will venture in, where wisdom ance hath been!
But I will doun yon river rove amang the wood sae green,
    And a' to pu a posie to my ain dear May!   *pluck, own*

The primrose I will pu, the firstling o the year,
And I will pu the pink, the emblem o my dear,
For she's the pink o womankind, and blooms without a peer –
    And a' to be a posie to my ain dear May!

I'll pu the budding rose, when Phoebus peeps in view,
For it's like a baumy kiss o her sweet, bonie mou.   *balmy, mouth*
The hyacinth's for constancy wi its unchanging blue –
    And a' to be a posie to my ain dear May!

The lily it is pure, and the lily it is fair,
And in her lovely bosom I'll place the lily there.
The daisy's for simplicity and unaffected air –
    And a' to be a posie to my ain dear May!

The hawthorn I will pu, wi its locks o siller gray,
Where, like an aged man, it stands at break o day;
But the songster's nest within the bush I winna tak away –   *will not*
    And a' to be a posie to my ain dear May!

The woodbine I will pu, when the e'ening star is near,
And the diamond draps o dew shall be her een sae clear!
The violet's for modesty, which weel she fa's to wear –
    And a' to be a posie to my ain dear May!

I'll tie the posie round wi the silken band o luve,
And I'll place it in her breast, and I'll swear by a' above,
That to my latest draught o life the band shall ne'er remove
    And this will be a posie to my ain dear May!

This is a charming love poem on the language of flowers. Much variety of pace and emphasis can be used. Lyric.

As I Stood by Yon Roofless Tower

As I stood by yon roofless tower,
  Where the wa'flow'r scents the dewy air,
Where the houlet mourns in her ivy bower,   owl
  And tells the midnight moon her care:

The winds were laid, the air was still,
  The stars they shot along the sky,
The tod was howling on the hill,   fox
  And the distant-echoing glens reply.

The burn, adown its hazelly path,   brook
  Was rushing by the ruin'd wa',
Hasting to join the sweeping Nith,
  Whase roaring seemed to rise and fa'.   Whose

The cauld blae North was streaming forth
  Her lights, wi hissing, eerie din:
Athort the lift they start and shift,   Athwart, horizon
  Like Fortune's favors, tint as win.   lost

Now, looking over firth and fauld,   fold
  Her horn the pale-faced Cynthia rear'd,   the moon
When lo! in form of minstrel auld
  A stern and stalwart ghaist appear'd.   ghost

And frae his harp sic strains did flow,   such
  Might rous'd the slumbering Dead to hear,
But O, it was a tale of woe,
  As ever met a Briton's ear!

He sang wi joy his former day,
  He, weeping, wail'd his latter times:
But what he said – it was nae play!
  I winna ventur't in my rhymes.

The ballad form – the style of speaking is narrative – that is tell a story.

Address to Edinburgh

Edina! Scotia's darling seat!
  All hail thy palaces and tow'rs,
Where once, beneath a Monarch's feet,
  Sat Legislation's sov'reign pow'rs:
From marking wildly-scatt'red flow'rs,
  As on the banks of Ayr I stray'd,
And singing, lone, the ling'ring hours,
  I shelter in thy honor'd shade.

Here Wealth still swells the golden tide,
  As busy Trade his labour plies;
There Architecture's noble pride
  Bids elegance and splendour rise:
Here Justice, from her native skies,
  High wields her balance and her rod;
There Learning, with his eagle eyes,
  Seeks Science in her coy abode.

Thy sons, Edina, social, kind,
  With open arms the stranger hail;
Their views enlarg'd, their lib'ral mind,
  Above the narrow, rural vale;
Attentive still to Sorrow's wail,
  Our modest Merit's silent claim:
And never may their sources fail!
  And never Envy blot their name!

Thy daughters bright thy walks adorn,
  Gay as the gilded summer sky,
Sweet as the dewy, milk-white thorn,
  Dear as the raptur'd thrill of joy!
Fair Burnet strikes th' adoring eye,   Eliza Burnett, Lord Monboddo's youngest daughter (1766-90)
  Heav'n's beauties on my fancy shine:
I see the Sire of Love on high,
  And own His work indeed divine!

There, watching high the least alarms,
  Thy rough, rude fortress gleams afar,
Like some bold vet'ran, grey in arms,
  And mark'd with many a seamy scar:
The pond'rous wall and massy bar,
  Grim-rising o'er the rugged rock,
Have oft withstood assailing war,
  And oft repell'd th' invader's shock.

With awe-struck thought and pitying tears,
  I view that noble, stately dome,
Where Scotia's kings of other years,
  Fam'd heroes! had their royal home:
Alas, how chang'd the times to come!
  Their royal name low in the dust!
Their hapless race wild-wand'ring roam!
  Tho rigid Law cries out, ''Twas just!'

Wild beats my heart to trace your steps,
  Whose ancestors, in days of yore,
Thro hostile ranks and ruin'd gaps
  Old Scotia's bloody lion bore:
Ev'n I, who sing in rustic lore,
  Haply my sires have left their shed,
And fac'd grim Dangers's loudest roar,
  Bold-following where your fathers led!

This poem must be addressed to Edinburgh and its castle personified. Narrative.

The Rights of Woman

An Occasional Address Spoken by Miss Fontenelle on Her Benefit Night, Nobember 26, 1792

While Europe's eye is fix'd on mighty things,
The fate of empires and the fall of kings;
While quacks of State must each produce his plan,
And even children lisp the Rights of Man;
Amid this mighty fuss just let me mention,
The Rights of Woman merit some attention.

First, in the sexes' intermix'd connexion,
One sacred Right of Woman is Protection:
The tender flower that lifts its head elate,
Helpless must fall before the blasts of fate,
Sunk on the earth, defac'd its lovely form,
Unless your shelter ward th' impending storm.

Our second Right – but needless here is caution –
To keep that right inviolate's the fashion:
Each man of sense has it so full before him,
He'd die before he'd wrong it – 'tis Decorum!

Louisa Fontenelle was an actress in the 18th century. She performed in the Theatre Royal when Burns was living in Dumfries. A poem for a girl. It demands a full delivery. Narrative.

There was, indeed, in far less polish'd days,
A time, when rough rude Man had naughty ways:
Would swagger, swear, get drunk, kick up a riot,
Nay, even thus invade a lady's quiet!
Now, thank our stars! these Gothic times are fled;
Now, well-bred men – and you are all well-bred –
Most justly think (and we are much the gainers)
Such conduct neither spirit, wit, nor manners.
For Right the third, our last, our best, our dearest:
That right to fluttering female hearts the nearest,
Which even the Rights of Kings, in low prostration,
Most humbly own – 'tis dear, dear Admiration!
In that blest sphere alone we live and move;
There taste that life of life – Immortal Love.
Smiles, glances, sighs, tears, fits, flirtations, airs –
'Gainst such an host what flinty savage dares?
When awful Beauty joins with all her charms,
Who is so rash as rise in rebel arms?
But truce with kings, and truce with constitutions,
With bloody armaments and revolutions;
Let Majesty your first attention summon,
Ah! ça ira! THE MAJESTY OF WOMAN!

French revolutionary slogan

The Twa Dogs

CAESAR

I've aften wonder'd, honest Luath,
What sort of life poor dogs like you have;
An when the gentry's life I saw,
What way poor bodies liv'd ava.   *at all*
    Our laird gets in his racked rents,   *paid in kind*
His coals, his kain, an a' his stents: *dues*
He rises when he likes himsel;
His flunkies answer at the bell;
He ca's his coach; he ca's his horse;
He draws a bonie silken purse,
As lang's my tail, whare, thro the steeks,   *stitches*
The yellow letter'd Geordie keeks.   *guinea, peeps*
    Frae morn to e'en it's nought but toiling,
At baking, roasting, frying, boiling;
An tho the gentry first are stechin,   *cramming*
Yet ev'n the ha' folk fill their pechan   *servants, stomach*
Wi sauce, ragouts, an sic like trashtrie   *rubbish*
That's little short o downright wastrie.   *wasteful*
Our whipper-in, wee, blastit wonner,   *Hugh Andrew, huntsman at Coilsfield*
Poor, worthless elf, it eats a dinner,
Better than onie tenant-man
His Honor has in a' the lan;
An what poor cot-folk pit their painch in,   *put, paunch*
I own it's past my comprehension.

Convey the mood of the rich not knowing how the poor live. Narrative.

Fair fa' your honest, sonsie face,   cheerful
Great chieftain o the puddin'-race!
Aboon them a' ye tak your place,   Above
    Painch, tripe, or thairm: paunch, guts
Weel are ye wordy of a grace   worthy
    As lang's my arm.

The groaning trencher there ye fill,
Your hurdies like a distant hill,   buttocks
Your pin wad help to mend a mill   skewer
    In time o need,
While thro your pores the dews distil
    Like amber bead.

His knife see rustic Labour dight,   wipe
An cut you up wi ready slight,   skill
Trenching your gushing entrails bright,   Diggin
    Like onie ditch;
And then, O what a glorious sight,
    Warm-reekin, rich!   -steaming

Then, horn for horn, they stretch an strive: spoon
Deil tak the hindmost, on they drive,
Till a' their well-swall'd kytes belyve   well-swollen bellies, soon
    Are bent like drums;
The auld Guidman, maist like to rive,   burst
    'Bethankit' hums.

Is there that wore his french *ragout*,
Or *olio* that wad staw a sow,   sicken
Or *fricassee* wad make her spew
    Wi perfect sconner,   disgust
Looks down wi sneering, scornfu view
    On sic a dinner?

Ye Pow'rs, wha mak mankind your care,
And dish them out their bill o fare,
Auld Scotland wants nae skinking ware   watery
    That jaups in luggies;   splashes, porringers
But, if ye wish her gratefu prayer,
    Gie her a Haggis!

When asked to recite this poem at a Burns Supper endeavour to give the right mood and emphasis to each verse.
A narrative address.

Auld Lang Syne

CHORUS
For auld lang syne, my dear   old long ago
   For auld lang syne,
We'll tak a cup o kindness yet,
   For auld lang syne!

Should auld acquaintance be forgot,
   And never brought to mind?
Should auld acquaintance be forgot,
   And auld lang syne?

And surely ye'll be your pint-stowp,   pay for, pint tankard
   And surely I'll be mine,
And we'll take a cup o kindness yet,
   For auld lang syne!

We twa hae run about the braes,   hillsides
   And pou'd the gowans fine,   pulled, daisies
But we've wander'd monie a weary fit,
   Sin auld lang syne.

We twa hae paidl'd in the burn   waded, stream
   Frae morning sun till dine,   noon, dinner-time
But seas between us braid hae roar'd   broad
   Sin auld lang syne.

And there's a hand my trusty fiere,   friend
   And gie's a hand o thine,
And we'll tak a right guide-willie waught,   goodwill drink
   For auld lang syne.

This poem is known the world over. It requires a note of remembrance.

A Burns Supper

A Burns supper was originally to celebrate the birthday of Robert Burns on the 25th of January. Nowadays it can be held at any time of the year although most take place in January or February.

To hold your own Burns supper you will need to invite your friends and make a list of who will sing, recite or make a short speech. Also decide on someone to be chairman.

The Supper

A Burns Supper, as the name implies, is a meal and this can be as simple or as elaborate as you like, but should include a haggis.

When everyone is seated the haggis is piped in, carried by a young member of the company. It is placed in front of the person who is to address the haggis. This is done by reciting 'To A Haggis' and using a knife to cut it open as described in the poem.

Grace is then said by the Chairman.

Some hae meat and canna eat,
And some wad eat that want it:
But we hae meat and we can eat,
Sae let the Lord be thankit.

The haggis is then served with 'tatties and neeps' either as the main course in the supper or alternatively as part of a more elaborate meal such as:–

Cock-a-Leekie Soup

Haggis, Neeps and Tatties

Main Course

Sweet

Bannocks & Cheese

Remember to keep some of your cola or lemonade for the toasts which are to follow the meal.

The Toasts

There is only one essential 'toast'. That is the toast to the Immortal Memory of Robert Burns, which should be a short speech about some aspect of Burns's life or his poems and songs. This should be the main speech.

Another toast 'To The Lassies' should be proposed by a laddie and replied to on behalf of the lassies – by a lassie of course. These should be light-hearted speeches.

Between toasts there should be recitation and songs and some community singing. A programme could be something like this:–

Toast	The Queen	Chairman
	All sing 'There Was A Lad'	
Toast	The Immortal Memory	Principal Speaker
	Song or Poem	
Toast	To The Lassies	A Lad
	Song or Poem	
	All sing 'Green Grow The Rashes O'	
Reply to the toast To The Lassies		A Lassie
	Song, Poem or Music	
Toast	The Chairman	A Lad
Vote of Thanks		A Lassie
	All sing 'Auld Lang Syne'	

112